*New Testament
Stories from the
Back Side*

New Testament Stories from the Back Side

J. ELLSWORTH KALAS

Abingdon Press
NASHVILLE

NEW TESTAMENT STORIES FROM THE BACK SIDE

This book is printed on acid-free paper.

Library of Congress Cataloging-in-Publication-Data

Kalas, J. Ellsworth, 1923-
  New Testament stories from the back side / J. Ellsworth Kalas.
    p. cm.
  ISBN 0-687-07306-5 (acid-free paper)
  1. Bible stories, English—N.T.   I. Title.

BS2400 .K35 2000
225.6—dc21
                                                                99-059768

Scripture quotations unless otherwise noted, are from the New Revised Standard Version Bible, copyright © 1989, by the Division of Christian Education of the National Council of the Churches of Christ in the United States of America.

Scripture quotations noted KJV are from the King James Version of the Bible.

Scripture quotations marked NLT are taken from the Holy Bible, New Living Translation, copyright © 1996. Used by permission of Tyndale House Publishers, Inc., Wheaton, Illinois 60189. All rights reserved.

Scripture quotations marked NIV® are taken from the HOLY BIBLE: NEW INTERNATIONAL VERSION. Copyright © 1973, 1978, 1984 by the International Bible Society. Used by permission of Zondervan Publishing House. All rights reserved.

02 03 04 05 06 07 08 09—10 9 8 7 6 5 4

MANUFACTURED IN THE UNITED STATES OF AMERICA

To
Jim Batten
Clarke Hoak
Ed McGrath
Dick Meadows
Bob Morey
Dick Reed
John Twist

"A friend loveth at all times,
and a brother is born for adversity."
PROVERBS 17:17 KJV

CONTENTS

INTRODUCTION

When I wrote *Old Testament Stories from the Back Side*, I knew that my problem was to interest readers in the obscure. I knew that not many would know the story of Jephthah and that although most people have heard of King David, they probably hadn't heard of his romance with Abigail. But because I loved the wonder of those stories, and the power of the truths they conveyed, I felt compelled to share them with readers.

My problem in *New Testament Stories from the Back Side* is the familiar. Many of these stories are so familiar that a reader may reason that there's no reason to read them, because he or she already knows everything about the story.

But in truth, there's always a danger that the familiar will become obscure. When something is familiar we allow it also to become ordinary. In time we forget how beautiful it is, until we lose touch with the original power of the story. I had a friend long ago who didn't realize how much he loved his former fiancée until he saw her on the arm of another man. The sight startled him so much that he sought her out the next day in order to reestablish their relationship. In time he married her, and they have, as the saying goes, lived happily ever after.

I hope, in this book, to let you see some old stories on the arm of a new insight; and I hope that the sight will cause you to fall in love with the old story all over again. If you do, this will be a book of worth.

J. Ellsworth Kalas

CHAPTER 1

Baby Pictures

LUKE 2:22-38: When the time came for their purification according to the law of Moses, they brought him up to Jerusalem to present him to the Lord (as it is written in the law of the Lord, "Every firstborn male shall be designated as holy to the Lord"), and they offered a sacrifice according to what is stated in the law of the Lord, "a pair of turtledoves or two young pigeons."

Now there was a man in Jerusalem whose name was Simeon; this man was righteous and devout, looking forward to the consolation of Israel, and the Holy Spirit rested on him. It had been revealed to him by the Holy Spirit that he would not see death before he had seen the Lord's Messiah. Guided by the Spirit, Simeon came into the temple; and when the parents brought in the child Jesus, to do for him what was customary under the law, Simeon took him in his arms and praised God, saying,

"Master, now you are dismissing
   your servant in peace,
   according to your word;
for my eyes have seen your salvation,
   which you have prepared in
   the presence of all peoples,
a light for revelation to the
   Gentiles
   and for glory to your people
   Israel."

And the child's father and mother were amazed at what was being said about him. Then Simeon blessed them and said to his mother Mary, "This child is destined for the falling and the rising of many in Israel, and to be a sign that will be opposed so that the inner thoughts of many will be revealed—and a sword will pierce your own soul too."

There was also a prophet, Anna the daughter of Phanuel, of the tribe of Asher. She was of a great age, having lived with her husband seven years after her marriage, then as a widow to the age of eighty-four. She never left the temple but worshiped there with fasting and prayer night and day. At that moment she came, and began to praise God and to speak about the child to all who were looking for the redemption of Jerusalem.

*M*any years ago, when I was a young pastor, I knew a man who was probably the proudest grandfather in captivity. He may have done more for Kodak stock than any person other than professional photographers. Almost every Sunday morning, as I came to the back of the church to greet people after worship, he was waiting for me, pictures in hand: the latest developments of his several grandchildren. You've heard of the man who said to his friend, "Have I shown you the most recent pictures of my grandchildren?"—and the friend answers, "No, and I want to thank you." I have a feeling that this long-ago friend of mine was the reason for that story.

Somehow he came to mind not long ago as I was reading the familiar Christmas story. For no particular reason, I asked myself what parents and grandparents did before cameras, before there were baby pictures. What, pray tell, did grandparents do? And what, specifically, did Joseph and Mary do?

And of course the answer came to me rather quickly. Before there were cameras, people took pictures with their eyes, developed them in their brains, and printed them with their tongues. For thousands of years, those were the only baby pictures anyone knew. A father's report in the village store was quite simple: "Our baby came last night. A boy. About so long. Big fellow; must weigh eight, maybe nine pounds. Just a little bit of hair. Got his mother's eyes."

Baby pictures. They're as old as the human race, and, in their own way, more graphic than anything a camera can record, because they leave so much room for the imagination of the one receiving the report.

Fortunately, we have such baby pictures of Jesus of Nazareth. Three, perhaps four, of them.

Luke gives us the earliest picture, one that was taken the night Jesus was born. Joseph and Mary had arrived in Bethlehem when Mary was late in her pregnancy. They couldn't find a room anywhere. Bethlehem was a one-street town, so the possibilities were always limited; but especially at this time, when people were returning to register for an empire-wide taxation. The town had a small, primitive hotel, but it was full to the limits. So Joseph and Mary found a place for themselves in a cave-stable, and just in time. When the baby was born, they used the only facility they had; they commandeered a manger for the crib.

The news of the birth spread in a remarkable way. Some shepherds who were tending their flocks in a nearby field were visited by an angel who told them of the birth. The shepherds, not surprisingly, decided to see for themselves. What they saw made such an impression on them that they told people all over Bethlehem, and these people were "amazed at what the shepherds told them" (Luke 2:18). Obviously, the shepherds took some good baby pictures. So good, come to think of it, that we still have them today.

The next picture also comes to us from Luke. When Jesus was just over a month old, Joseph and Mary took him to the temple for a special Jewish ritual. I think it is fair to say that what happened that day was much like an infant baptism or dedication in our day. So of course we're not surprised that some pictures were taken. In one of the pictures, an old man, Simeon, is holding the baby in his arms, and he's praying. In another, a devout eighty-four-year-old woman, Anna, is praising God for the child. Of all the grandparents, uncles, aunts, and godparents who have ever been photographed with a baby, none could have been more awestruck than these two who came, providentially, upon the scene.

Matthew took the third picture. I'm not sure where to place it; it was taken either just before the picture I've just described, or very soon after. In any event, when the baby

Jesus was still very small, a little company of wise men came to where the family was staying. These wise men had made a remarkable journey to get to the baby. When they saw him, they presented him with gifts—gold, frankincense, and myrrh. Look long at this snapshot, because it is quite impressive: A tiny Jewish baby with a group of learned, rather powerful men from another part of the world. It's a quite different picture from the one where the baby was surrounded by shepherds.

Perhaps by now you've noticed something peculiar about these baby pictures. They don't reveal any of the details we look for in baby pictures, whether those pictures come by camera or by word of mouth or announcement. We don't know how much the baby weighed, or his length in inches. The pictures don't tell us the color of his hair, or anything about his features. The only physical detail we receive is about his wardrobe. We're told that Joseph and Mary wrapped him in a swaddling cloth. This was a large square of cloth with a long strip, like a bandage, coming off one corner. A child was wrapped in the cloth, then the long strip was wound around and around, to secure the covering. And that's the only thing we know about the physical appearance of the baby Jesus—just the way he was wrapped when the shepherds found him. The astonishing thing is this: As far as we know, that's the way every baby in that part of the world was wrapped in those days. So when the angel told the shepherds that the baby would be wrapped this way, it was like saying, "He will appear entirely ordinary." How will you recognize him? Because he will look the way babies always look!

But Jesus' baby pictures don't tell us if he was little or big, hairy or bald. We don't know if he was cute (that seems to be the question we always ask about babies), or if he appeared rather average.

And, come to think of it, we have no details about Jesus' physical appearance at any point in his life. In numbers of other instances the Bible tells us something of how people looked. We know that Zacchaeus was short, and that King Saul was head and shoulders taller than the average person. We know that the prophet Elisha was bald, and that young David was ruddy and handsome. But we don't know a thing, not a single thing, about the physical appearance of Jesus. Isn't that astonishing? Here is the person who has been depicted by artists more than any other person in human history, yet the Bible doesn't give us the least hint about his physical appearance.

So what do Jesus' baby pictures tell us? Or, for that matter, what do the later pictures tell us?

They tell us *not* what he looked like, but who he *is*.

Think of that first picture, the one taken on the night Jesus was born. The angel that came to the shepherds told them, "I am bringing you good news of great joy for all the people," because a *Savior* had been born, and he was "Christ the Lord." And then, a peculiar sort of letdown: you will find him in a manger (Is that any place to find a *Savior*?), and he will be dressed the way every baby is dressed, in a swaddling cloth! You would think that a Savior, the Christ of God, would be dressed in rays of light, or at least in the extravagance of a king. But God is saying that if Jesus is to be the Savior, he will have to be like every one of us. His most distinguishing feature is that he is not distinguished at all. He is a baby, like every person that was ever born. By this unique ordinariness, he can be the Savior to every person who is ever born.

The second picture has the same quality. Jesus is brought to the temple to have a typical Jewish experience, to be presented before God just as was every Jewish boy born in those days. Again, it was as if the photographer were saying that this is a baby like every other baby, experiencing what every Jewish baby experiences.

And yet, different. Utterly different. Remember that the shepherds get the word of Jesus' birth not through village gossip, but through an angel, and then a whole chorus of angels. So also when Joseph and Mary bring Jesus to the temple for a customary ritual, they are suddenly joined by an old man, Simeon, and an old woman, Anna, who have been waiting years for this very day, although they had no idea what sort of day it would be. Simeon dares to take the child from Joseph and Mary, and prophesies over him. Then Anna begins to give ecstatic thanks for the baby, and to tell everyone about him. So it is that this customary ritual suddenly takes on cosmic proportions. And of course, the visit of the wise men is quite special. It says that this baby— this baby born in such humble circumstances, who doesn't seem especially photogenic—matters to the whole world, so that some rather distinguished foreigners travel for weeks to honor him.

I mentioned earlier that there are three, perhaps four, baby pictures of Jesus. We often miss the fourth. You will find it in John's collection. We miss it because it is so unlike any usual baby pictures. It begins with the moment of conception; not when Jesus was conceived in the womb of Mary, but when the plan itself was conceived. "In the beginning was the Word," John says. And then, the baby picture: "And the Word became flesh and lived among us" (John 1:14). Now *there's* a picture for your photo album! It's as if a camera had captured a ray of light beyond the reach of the human eye, or a device had recorded a sound outside the reach of a human ear.

So what does all of this have to do with Christmas? Everything, everything! You and I are always looking for baby pictures of Jesus. That is, we want Christmas to be a sentimental time. Now, mind you, there's nothing wrong with sentiment. I'm obligated to say that, because I am *myself* a prince of sentiment. But sentiment has its place and its limits, and it has gone beyond its place when it begins to fence in the profound wonder and truth of Christmas.

That is, we dare not let Christmas be lost in cards and gifts, in parties and in meeting with old friends, or even in the-whole-family-getting-together-again. Good and wonderful as these things are, they aren't really what Christmas is about. Indeed, we dare not even lose Christmas in music and pageants, and in talk about world peace. For although these things are beautiful and praiseworthy, they are extensions of Christmas, and not its heart.

Because, you see, Jesus didn't come to give us a sentimental holiday; he came to save us from sin. He didn't come because we are nice people, but because we are lost people; and because if he hadn't come, we could never be found. If we let "Merry Christmas" become simply "Season's Greetings," and if the *holy* day becomes just a holiday—well, it will be as if the shepherds leaving the manger had told their friends, "We've just seen the cutest little baby boy!" and as if the wise men had sent a congratulatory letter rather than traveling weeks in order to bring their gold, frankincense, and myrrh.

The baby pictures of Jesus that Matthew, Luke, and John give us don't tell us anything about the way the baby looked—perhaps to our disappointment, because we'd like so much to have a visual image. But they do tell us who Jesus was and is, the very Son of God, and our Savior. And they tell us why he came. He came because you and I, and everyone we know, were absolutely hopeless, and because there wasn't a chance in time or eternity that we could ever be right.

Now in saying that, I may very well have ruined your image of Christmas. Indeed, you may be ready to identify me as something of a Grinch stealing Christmas, because I've delivered some bad news—the fact that, short of God's intervention, we are hopeless—when we prefer at Christmastime to have as many fuzzy and uncomplicated feelings as possible. And yet, in truth, every one of us knows that Christmas is *not* that simple. Not as *we* experience it. Because our Christmas celebrations are always intruded upon by some very "unChristmas" feelings—feelings, for some, of bereavement, or lost friends or relationships; and for others, of sickness or loneliness or wistful memories of Christmas past. All of which is to say that our human scene

17

is quite hopeless unless God intervenes to heal it. And that's where Christmas comes in. It is so much more, you see, than a pleasant, passing feeling of sentiment. It is the story of eternal salvation.

That's why I wanted to tell you about Jesus' baby picture. The picture is so much more than the beguiling recital of physical characteristics that we usually look for in our pictures, and so much more than the warm pictures that sentiment tries to paint at the Christmas season. It is not a picture of how Jesus *looked*, but who he *was*. And that, of course, is because what you and I need is not a charming or even a dramatically powerful figure; we need a Savior.

Don't settle for less in your Christmas baby picture. Because to settle for less is to miss Christmas altogether.

CHAPTER 2

Mary Shouldn't Have Worried

LUKE 2:39-51: When they had finished everything required by the law of the Lord, they returned to Galilee, to their own town of Nazareth. The child grew and became strong, filled with wisdom; and the favor of God was upon him.

Now every year his parents went to Jerusalem for the festival of the Passover. And when he was twelve years old, they went up as usual for the festival. When the festival was ended and they started to return, the boy Jesus stayed behind in Jerusalem, but his parents did not know it. Assuming that he was in the group of travelers, they went a day's journey. Then they started to look for him among their relatives and friends. When they did not find him, they returned to Jerusalem to search for him. After three days they found him in the temple, sitting among the teachers, listening to them and asking them questions. And all who heard him were amazed at his understanding and his answers. When his parents saw him they were astonished; and his mother said to him, "Child, why have you treated us like this? Look, your father and I have been searching for you in great anxiety." He said to them, "Why were you searching for me? Did you not know that I must be in my Father's house?" But they did not understand what he said to them. Then he went down with them and came to Nazareth, and was obedient to them. His mother treasured all these things in her heart.

*Y*ou don't have to be very religious to be curious about the childhood of Jesus. Anyone who is a modest student of our human story can hardly help wondering about the thirty years of Jesus' life from the time of his birth until the beginning of his brief, three-year ministry. After all, Jesus became the most influential person ever to walk on our planet. We testify to this fact each time we glance at the calendar or a digital watch, because we divide our human history into B.C. and A.D. on the basis of Jesus' birth. Nor is the point changed by the contemporary effort to substitute B.C.E. (before the Common Era) and C.E. (Common Era). In a strange sort of way, these new letters only accentuate the point: The birth of Jesus has indeed established what is now "common" to our human story—although, in truth, the common has come to us in a most *un*common way.

No wonder we can't help pondering what people and events shaped the life of Jesus in his growing-up years. All of us who love biographies want to know the experiences that might have influenced Jesus in what modern psychology would call the formative years of his life. Besides, when a biography covers only some thirty-three years, as is the case with Jesus, if the years between two and thirty are silent, our curiosity is all the more piqued.

Then, too, there's a *sentimental* part of us that wants to hear stories from Jesus' boyhood years. We'd like to have a few fitting sequels to the angel song the shepherds heard, and the awesome visit of the wise men. We want some heart-warming scenes, with just a touch of the miraculous—the sort of anecdotes that would make good church pageants, the kind we could use for Mother's Day or Children's Day.

But the biblical writers didn't do us any such favors. They tell us about Jesus' birth, including the sacred rites in the temple; about the frantic trip his parents made to Egypt in order to escape Herod's wrath; and about Jesus' return at age two to the family home in Nazareth. But then, nothing more until Jesus is thirty years old and leaving home to teach and preach. Nothing about his boyhood, youth, or early manhood. Except, that is, for one brief incident, something that happened when he was twelve years old.

The story begins in a quite ordinary way. When a Jewish

boy reached the age of twelve, he was qualified to enter the adult religious world, and thus to be part of the ceremonial trips to Jerusalem for the high holy days. So in Jesus' twelfth year, he went with his parents to Jerusalem for the festival of the Passover. When the celebration had ended, Joseph and Mary set out on their homeward journey, not knowing that Jesus had stayed behind in Jerusalem. They assumed Jesus was with others of their Nazareth contingent, and they traveled for a day in the slow, laborious fashion of the times before they realized that their son was not with them. Concerned, they went back to Jerusalem to continue the search. Three increasingly anxious days later, Joseph and Mary found Jesus "in the temple, sitting among the teachers, listening to them and asking them questions" (Luke 2:46).

Luke tells us that the temple conversation between Jesus and the scholars was causing quite a stir among the listeners. People were "amazed" at Jesus' understanding and the answers he was giving. How was it that a lad from the hill country had such a grasp of the scriptures that he could converse on challenging terms with men who had spent their whole lives mastering the sacred documents?

Jesus' mother, however, saw things simply from a motherly point of view. "Child," she said, "why have you treated us like this? Look, your father and I have been searching for you in great anxiety" (Luke 2:48). Any parent who reads this story sympathizes with Mary. But Jesus' reply is quite matter-of-fact. "Why were you searching for me? Did you not know that I must be in my Father's house?" (Luke 2:49).

As I have previously said, this event is really not too spectacular. Not as much so, at any rate, as we may wish it had been. There were no fireworks, no angel voices, no dramatic healings or evidences of divine intervention. The only feature of this story that makes a particular impression on most of us is actually just a cultural peculiarity. We find it hard to imagine leaving a twelve-year-old behind and not realizing it until the next day. But that, I repeat, is a cultural thing. On the one hand, a boy of twelve was considered a man in that day; that's why Jesus was attending this festival, as a celebration of his majority. And, of course, first-century Jerusalem was not like twentieth-century Chicago, New York, Los Angeles, or London. There were hazards, of course, but they can hardly be compared to the urban perils of our time.

Furthermore, in that first century world they really did feel that a child belonged to the whole village. Everyone watched out for everyone else's children. Few of us can imagine such a world today (although such communities still exist, not only in much of the developing world, but in many places in small-town America).

What shall we make of Jesus' encounter with the teachers in the temple? Luke wants us to know that something special happened. Those teachers were probably the brightest and best in all the land. We are impressed, as were the onlookers, that the twelve-year-old Jesus is so engaged in conversation with them. But is the story meant simply to impress us that Jesus was a very precocious child with a high I.Q.? If so, it is the kind of anecdote that can be found in hundreds of records of the great and near great. Indeed, it's the sort of thing you've heard reported in dinner conversations or family reunions, or have found in not too condensed form in someone's annual Christmas letter.

Surely there's more to the story than that. If the aim of the story is to impress us with Jesus' powers—well, surely there must have been something in those thirty silent years that would have been more strikingly characteristic.

Unless, perhaps, Luke isn't trying to impress us with Jesus' boyish genius. Might Luke be giving us a preview of the showdown some twenty years later, when some of these same scholars, grown older, or their official descendants, challenge Jesus on the streets with questions they hope will impale him? Is the writer suggesting that someday the exchange between Jesus and the temple leaders will no longer be benign?

Or does Luke want us to realize that Jesus already grasped, at twelve, his divine mission: "Did you not know that I must be in my Father's house?" (Luke 2:49)—or, as the footnote translation puts it, "must be about my Father's interests?" If so, what more significant time to announce it than on the occasion of Jesus' entrance into spiritual maturity! One thinks, too, of the language John's Gospel uses in describing Jesus: "The Lamb of God who takes away the sin of the world" (John 1:29). The sacrificial lamb was the most poignant emblem of the Passover, the celebration that had brought Jesus to Jerusalem with Joseph and Mary. Is this Jesus' special role in his Father's house?

But I digress. I am fascinated with the matter-of-fact quality in Jesus' response to his mother. Mary has said that she and Joseph had suffered "great anxiety," and the parent in me nods agreement. But when you put Jesus' answer in the simplest terms, he was saying, "Why were you worried? Why were you looking at large? Where else would you have expected to find me except here?"

Like so many Bible stories, this one no doubt has several layers of meaning. These stories so often interweave the routine and the breathtaking without pausing for an explanation or without bothering to differentiate between the several layers. After all, the whole Bible is concerned with the story of God's relationship to our human race, so why shouldn't we expect that the temporal and the eternal might intersect at this point too?

Usually we need to be reminded that there is an eternal element in the human story. But in this case—probably because we're looking for a miracle worthy of the Bible's only anecdote of Jesus' boyhood—we have to remind ourselves of the human elements the story contains.

There's an inference, it seems to me, in Jesus' answer to his mother. It goes like this: For twelve years you have raised me to be a certain kind of person, with a particular set of values. Considering the way I've been raised, where else would I be but in God's house? Why did it take you three

23

days to locate me? Basic logic should have told you where I could be found. Mother, you shouldn't have worried.

Generations earlier a wisdom writer had said,

> Train children in the right way,
> and when old, they will not
> stray.   (PROVERBS 22:6)

Everything we know about Mary and Joseph persuades us that they raised Jesus in the godliest of homes. We can never fully know the degree to which they understood Jesus' eternal mission. True, they had received revelation before his birth and confirmation at times afterward. But we human beings are in some ways very earthbound, and we find it difficult to hold on to even the most substantial of verities. But Mary and Joseph were good people, thoroughly God-fearing; that's why they were chosen, and that's why they responded at the outset as they did. So we can be sure that they raised Jesus with the highest religious values. Now, Jesus was paying them a matter-of-fact compliment: Where else would you expect to find me but in the midst of the values with which you have raised me?

This story is both reassuring and frightening. All things considered, we can expect to find children at a logical destination. Yes, there seem at times to be painful exceptions. In my nearly forty years as a parish pastor, I've known some good people whose children didn't seem to follow their parents' course. I have no desire to pass judgment in any such instances.

But the basic rule is clear. Children don't get lost, they wind up where—knowingly or not—we have directed them. In general, when parents are called to meet a son or a daughter in a police station, they might well hear a voice saying, "Where else did you expect to find him?" Or to get closer to a larger number of us, we know that we should expect to find our children in a shopping mall, because we've raised them with unceasing lessons in materialism and acquisitiveness. And a great many of us ought not to be surprised if our children end up thoroughly materialistic, with no goal in life other than to be "successful," whatever that may mean. Where else but in the rat race should we expect to find them when we've raised them as some of us have?

Of course, Mary and Joseph had an easier job of it than do parents in the twenty-first century. Today, parents have to be more intentional about their goals than did first-century parents, because parents must now contend with teachers who may negate the parental influence on every hand—teachers like television and the Internet. Perhaps other generations could have dared to say, "My children know how I feel without my spelling it out to them," but such a laissez-faire attitude will no longer work. The competition for the human soul is much too fierce for that. When one thinks of the number of subtle and corrupting siren voices that solicit a child or a teenager, one is astonished that so many children turn out as well as they do. The quiet wooing of the Holy Spirit and what theologians call prevenient grace—the faithfulness of God that seeks us before we turn heavenward—are more active in our world than we can ever estimate, else the cause of righteousness would be quite overwhelmed by the never-ceasing insistence of the secular, the easy, the immediately profitable or enjoyable.

Nevertheless, the main burden of influence rests upon us, the parents and surrogate parents. That is, we parents, teachers, employers, neighbors, and godly friends are the ones who determine whether a new generation will be found in the temple or in the provinces of shallow, thoughtless, and destructive living. And because shallow or thoughtless living doesn't seem as perilous as "destructive" living, we may need to remind ourselves that life's perils often come in comfortable clothing.

Well, I'm back to where I began, marveling that the Bible tells us so little about the years between Jesus' birth and his short ministry. And it's especially interesting that the only story we've been given is an account of Jesus as a boy of twelve, in what is hardly more than a lovely little family anecdote. It isn't the kind of miracle story that many would want. There is little fanfare, really. Luke tells us that Jesus went back to Nazareth with Joseph and Mary, and that he "was obedient to them" (Luke 2:51). True, Mary "treasured all these things in her heart," but basically, life returned to normal.

But what a lesson there is in the normal, when the normal is *right*. Because when the normal is right, we can justifiably expect that things will turn out right. So Jesus could say, in effect, you raised me to honor the house of God, the people of God, and the law of God. So if you don't know where I am, you can nevertheless be sure that I will be where your teachings have led me.

Mary shouldn't have worried. Jesus was precisely where her twelve years of influence had predictably led him.

CHAPTER 3

Listen to the Wind

JOHN 3:1-8: Now there was a Pharisee named Nicodemus, a leader of the Jews. He came to Jesus by night and said to him, "Rabbi, we know that you are a teacher who has come from God; for no one can do these signs that you do apart from the presence of God." Jesus answered him, "Very truly, I tell you, no one can see the kingdom of God without being born from above." Nicodemus said to him, "How can anyone be born after having grown old? Can one enter a second time into the moth-er's womb and be born?" Jesus answered, "Very truly, I tell you, no one can enter the kingdom of God without being born of water and Spirit. What is born of the flesh is flesh, and what is born of the Spirit is spirit. Do not be aston-ished that I said to you, 'You must be born from above.' The wind blows where it chooses, and you hear the sound of it, but you do not know where it comes from or where it goes. So it is with every-one who is born of the Spirit."

I have lived in the world of religion since before I was born, and in this long period of observation I have learned two things for sure: First, that we can't box God in; and second, that we are always trying to do so.

Let me interrupt myself long enough to comment on my opening statement, that I have lived in the world of religion since before I was born. The psalmist said that God knew him when he was still in his mother's womb (Psalm 139:13). In my case, my mother made sure that this was so. When she learned that she was with child, at a point in her life when she preferred not to be, she sought to bargain with God. Since she already had a supply of daughters, she promised God that if this baby were a boy, she would give him to the ministry. So I am not speaking idly when I say that I have lived in the world of religion since before I was born.

I repeat, I have learned that we can't box God in. But we keep trying to put boundaries around our Lord. We insist that God follow ways that we approve of. No wonder, then, that when we come across places in the biblical story that don't appeal to us, we discard them with a philosophical wave of the hand. "God isn't like that," we say—as if we are the ones chosen to determine the nature of God. Scholars often complain about anthropomorphism in religion; that is, that we create gods in our own image. Ironically, scholars themselves are often guilty of doing so, as they decide how much of the biblical portrayal they will choose to endorse. Unhappy with the divine image they find in the scriptures, they opt for a divinity more in their own perceived image.

But we're all like that in some measure. It seems to me that it was true of a man nearly twenty centuries ago. He was a notably good human being. He was, in fact, intentionally good. That is, he was a Pharisee; and whatever else you might say about the Pharisees, you have to acknowledge that they didn't leave goodness to chance. They worked at it; it was their primary commitment. Perhaps it isn't surprising, therefore, that this man was confident he knew what God was like. Good people (or people who think themselves to be good, whether they are or not) may be especially inclined to have a rigid definition of what God is like.

So when this man—we'll call him Nicodemus, since that was his name—came to Jesus, there was a fascinating exchange. Let me put it in shorthand:

Nicodemus: Good evening. I admire you.
Jesus: You must be born again.
Nicodemus: That's impossible.
Jesus: Listen to the wind.

The conversation is really almost that stark. But let me give it to you in more detail, with some commentary. Nicodemus was not the sort of man who was likely to come to Jesus. He was a recognized leader among the Jews. The Jewish people didn't have much influence in those days, since they were subject to Rome, but Nicodemus walked the halls of whatever power existed in their small house. He was a scholar, a gentleman, and a force to be reckoned with. Jesus, on the other hand, was to all appearances lacking in credentials. He came from a backward part of the country, a community that was a natural butt of jokes. Nevertheless, miracles were beginning to attend his ministry, and growing crowds were coming to hear him teach.

So Nicodemus sought him out. He came to Jesus by night, perhaps partly because he didn't want to be seen with the Galilean teacher, and partly because nightfall was the ideal time for serious scholarly conversation. He approached Jesus with admirable gentility: "Rabbi, we know that you are a teacher who has come from God; for no one can do these signs that you do apart from the presence of God" (John 3:2).

Jesus didn't choose to engage in this kind of genteel Ping Pong. His answer seems abrupt almost to the point of discourtesy. "Very truly, I tell you, no one can see the kingdom of God without being born from above" (John 3:3).

It's at this point that Nicodemus puts his fences around God. I don't think he consciously intends to. It's just that he has his prejudices regarding what God can do or how much God intervenes in human affairs; which is to say, Nicodemus has his preconceptions about what God is like. As Nicodemus sees it, God doesn't get into such miracle activities as rebirths.

Jesus counters that in order to enter the kingdom of God we have to be born of both water and Spirit. "What is born of the flesh is flesh, and what is born of the Spirit is spirit" (John 3:6). This shouldn't be too hard to understand, Jesus suggests. Then he says, "The wind blows where it chooses, and you hear the sound of it, but you do not know where it comes from or where it goes. So it is with everyone who is born of the Spirit" (John 3:8).

Listen to the wind, Nicodemus. Listen to the wind.

Again and again, in both the Old and New Testaments, God's Spirit—the Holy Spirit—is described as being like the wind. Both the Hebrew of the Old Testament *(ruach)* and the Greek of the New Testament *(pneuma)* employ a word that can mean wind, breath, or spirit. When the writer of Genesis explains our divine origins, he tells us that God breathed into the human nostrils the *breath* of life (Genesis 2:7); that is, God *inspirited* us. When the Holy Spirit entered our world in a new way on the Day of Pentecost, one of the manifestations of the Spirit's coming was "a sound like the rush of a violent wind" that filled the house where the believers were sitting (Acts 2:2). Even so, when Jesus wanted Nicodemus to understand how he could be born from above, Jesus said that it was like the wind. You might not understand it, and certainly you couldn't control it, but you could feel its reality.

When the Bible pictures the Spirit of God as wind, it may well suggest several things. But surely it is saying that we can't put God in a box. We can't regularize or systemize God. We can't predict God or the divine activity. The television meteorologist offers a forecast each evening. We watch numerous impressive billows and streams that flow across the screen, telling us much of what we don't understand and even more that isn't our issue, since we want simply to know if we'll have rain tomorrow. But one thing we know for sure: Even though meteorology is a well-founded science, under constant examination and development, we still can speak with little certainty about air currents and wind factors. And if this is true of the wind of nature, which has some measurable elements, what shall we say about the wind of the Spirit?

Am I suggesting that the Holy Spirit of God is capricious or irresponsible? Not at all! It's just that we don't understand it; and perhaps, at a certain point, we're not supposed to, or are simply incapable of doing so. Life has many mysteries, some of which we live with intimately every day, so we shouldn't be surprised that the work of God's Spirit is beyond our total grasp. In fact, there's a sense in which if we could fully grasp God and God's dealings, we would be bigger than God, because we would have encompassed him. No, we needn't be surprised that the activities of God's Spirit are only partially and dimly perceived and understood.

Listen to the wind! C. S. Lewis was probably the most articulate defender of the Christian faith in the latter half of the twentieth century. But he was an atheist when he set off on a weekend holiday during his university years. He purchased a novel from the kiosk in the railroad station for reading during his trip. It was a novel by George MacDonald, chosen haphazardly. But as Lewis read, he later reported, his imagination was converted; the rest of him would follow later. How strange that the Wind would blow through a novel one might buy at a railroad newsstand!

But that wasn't all. Though Lewis had now acknowledged the existence of God, he did not believe in the primary essential of the Christian faith, that Jesus Christ is the Son of God. Then one sunny morning, while being driven to Whipsnade on a motorcycle by a friend, Lewis set out not believing in Jesus Christ, but "when we reached the zoo I did." It wasn't the product of thought, though Lewis was a scholar; nor was it, he says, a matter of great emotion. "It was more like when a man, after long sleep, still lying motionless in bed, becomes aware that he is now awake" (*Surprised by Joy*, 237). Listen to the Wind! You have no idea from whence it has come or where it is going. But you feel it, and you cannot deny its reality.

I remember a long-ago student at the University of Wisconsin. He began attending worship services at the church where I was the pastor—not out of regard for me, goodness knows, but because his girlfriend had become a

Christian and he felt obligated to give a hearing to her beliefs. But the young man was an agnostic at best, and probably an atheist. One week we conversed in my study for an intense hour. Although he listened attentively, he was not convinced.

But on a Sunday not long after, while I waited to process with the choir, the young man whispered to me that he was now a believer. How did it happen? Earlier that week, he had been reading one of the popular nihilistic philosophers when suddenly, without warning, he began to see the absurdity of all he was reading, and the magnificent truth of the God he had been rejecting. How do you explain such a change, against all logical odds? Well, explain the breeze that just passed by. So a person is proceeding rather blithely along familiar routines when suddenly there is the arresting of a reminiscent fragrance, a melody—not necessarily religious—that acts like some lost chord of the soul, a face that recalls a Sunday school teacher long gone, and at that moment, years of resistance begin to crumble. Listen to the Wind!

But let me be quick to confess that a person can, indeed, shut the wind out. One can hide behind walls of willfulness until, in time, the Spirit's breath can no longer be felt. Not because the Spirit is unable to break down our walls of resistance, but because the Spirit won't. No one in heaven or on earth is so respectful of the integrity of human personality as is the Spirit of God. God's Spirit will plead but will not demand. The Spirit is not a bully, but a Lover; and while that love pursues passionately, it will not intrude where it is not wanted; after all, if it did, it would cease to be love.

So if we want to, we can shut out the Wind. Jesus spoke of the "unpardonable sin," the sin against the Holy Spirit. Could it be that this sin which is beyond pardon is the sin of resisting the Spirit so long that one can no longer feel the Spirit's blowing? Perhaps so. After all, one can live with any sound for so long that one no longer really hears it. Perhaps that's what some have done to the Wind of God's Spirit.

Though the Wind is graciously insistent, we can be so stubbornly irresponsive as to shut out its influence.

As for Nicodemus, the sophisticated scholar and power broker, the Wind got to him. The record of the experience touches down at intervals in the Gospel story like a playful breeze. The next time we hear of Nicodemus is some indeterminate period later. He is with the group of leaders to whom he so rightly belongs. The group is trying to decide how to deal with the rising popularity of the Nazarene preacher Jesus. They're looking for an excuse to arrest him. But Nicodemus raises a question. "Our law does not judge people without first giving them a hearing to find out what they are doing, does it?" (John 7:51). It was a reasonable question, nothing more than a pursuit of fairness. But it was the only quiet voice raised in Jesus' defense, and the others resented it so much that they mocked Nicodemus for even suggesting another point of view.

I wonder if Nicodemus knew that the Wind was blowing even as he raised the question. Still more, I wonder how faithfully the Wind had blown in Nicodemus's soul for weeks or months prior to that minor but significant showdown with his associates.

Then, Jesus was crucified. It would seem that logic and fear would now quiet the Wind that had pursued Nicodemus. He could conclude that Jesus was not, as he had thought, a prophet sent from God, since he had been tried, condemned, and crucified. And he could surely have decided that it was better to be done with the whole matter before he endangered his standing with his colleagues of the inner circle.

But when Joseph of Arimathea took Jesus' body to a place of burial, there was Nicodemus, wooed by the Wind, helping Joseph wrap the scarred body in linen cloths, lavishing it with burial spices fit for a king. As the two men carried on their furtive burial of a man who had been executed as an enemy of the state, paying late homage to what must have seemed a hopeless cause, did Nicodemus recall a voice saying, "The wind blows where it chooses"? If so, he must have whispered to himself, "How true, how true!"

So listen to the Wind, the wonderful Wind of God. Step into its warmth, its embrace, its sometimes terrifying power. But be careful! If you want to stay as you are, running your own affairs and following your own fumbling ways, watch out, because the Wind woos and intrudes. But Oh, what a glory the Wind brings! What unpredictable, magnificent, eternal excitement! Don't try to box God in. It really doesn't work. Just listen to the Wind.

CHAPTER 4

In Defense of a Man I Don't Like

JOHN 5:2-16: Now in Jerusalem by the Sheep Gate there is a pool, called in Hebrew Bethzatha, which has five porticoes. In these lay many invalids—blind, lame, and paralyzed. One man was there who had been ill for thirty-eight years. When Jesus saw him lying there and knew that he had been there a long time, he said to him, "Do you want to be made well?" The sick man answered him, "Sir, I have no one to put me into the pool when the water is stirred up; and while I am making my way, someone else steps down ahead of me." Jesus said to him, "Stand up, take your mat and walk." At once the man was made well, and he took up his mat and began to walk.

Now that day was a sabbath. So the Jews said to the man who had been cured, "It is the sabbath; it is not lawful for you to carry your mat." But he answered them, "The man who made me well said to me, 'Take up your mat and walk.'" They asked him, "Who is the man who said to you, 'Take it up and walk'?" Now the man who had been healed did not know who it was, for Jesus had disappeared in the crowd that was there. Later Jesus found him in the temple and said to him, "See, you have been made well! Do not sin any more, so that nothing worse happens to you." The man went away and told the Jews that it was Jesus who had made him well. Therefore the Jews started persecuting Jesus, because he was doing such things on the sabbath.

I once asked an attorney of deep Christian conscience how he could defend a client in whose claim he did not really believe. "I remind myself," he said, "my role is that of an attorney, not that of a judge."

That's my situation at this moment. I'm about to discuss a person who doesn't naturally appeal to me. Something about his personality is less than admirable; and while it is true that all of us have our faults, it is also true that some faults are easier to live with than others. That's why the late Adela Rogers St. John recommended that we choose our friends for their faults, because it is important that they be faults we can live with. Well, this man's faults are the kind I would rather not be around.

Nevertheless, I believe that everyone has a right to a spirited defense, so I'm taking on this case that is unappealing to me. In truth, I'm probably trying more to convince myself than to convince you. No matter; my effort is sincere.

Let me tell you the story. In Jesus' time there was in Jerusalem a pool that was legendary for reported miraculous powers. Some said that an angel came "at certain seasons" (though it appears no one knew when these seasons would be) to stir the waters, and the person (or perhaps even persons) who stepped into the water first after such a stirring would be healed. As stories of these miracles grew, more and more people were brought to this place—persons who could not see, persons who could not walk, and persons who were ill with disease. Apparently some of the sick were accompanied by relatives or friends who could help rush them into the pool at the strategic moment. And while the sick who waited at the pool must have established a kind of camaraderie of need, they probably lost all sense of mutual caring in the ecstatic moment of a potential miracle. At that point all that mattered was to get into the water before the next person, even if a moment earlier one had looked upon that person as a fellow sufferer.

At that pool lay the man I'm trying to defend. I don't know how long he had been there; John's Gospel says simply that it had been "a long time" (John 5:6). We do know that he had been ill for thirty-eight years. And since the writer doesn't say that he was ill from birth, we may assume that his illness had come upon him at some point in his life.

Nor are we told the specific nature of his illness. We know that he was there on a mat, and that when Jesus healed him, it was with the command that he should take up his mat and walk, so we reason that his illness probably had something to do with his ability to walk. If his illness was the result of some sort of stroke or paralysis, it seems likely that he was at least a young man by the time it happened; and this suggests that he may have been in his later fifties or early sixties at this point in the Scriptures. If that is the case, he had exceeded the average life expectancy for a person in that first-century world.

But it must have been a dreary existence. Thirty-eight years of invalidism, not in a world like ours, where you are encouraged to find self sustenance and there are the means to do so, but a life in which your only choices were to beg or to live off the charity of family and friends. And if this man had ever had such family and friends, these supporters were apparently gone by now; or at the least, they were unable or unwilling to accompany him to the pool. He lay there alone and frustrated.

At this point I feel sorry for him, and you may too. I cannot really imagine being an invalid for thirty-eight years. And I surely cannot imagine being wholly dependent on other people for so long. I have an unduly strong independent streak, such that during my own two experiences of adult hospitalization, I twice incurred the rebuke of nurses (second only to the wrath of elementary school teachers) for doing things that (they hinted) only an idiot would try to do. No, I can't imagine being ill and helpless for the larger share of one's adult life. So I sympathize with him.

I wonder, too, what such an experience does to a person's spirit? The wise writer said that hope deferred makes the heart sick (Proverbs 13:12). How long can a person wait with dreams unanswered before he or she loses heart? How many times can you reach for the gold and come up empty before you stop reaching? I wonder if this man now stayed by the pool not because he really expected some day to be healed, but because his staying there provided some element of defense—perhaps like a person who has been out of work for several years and who now applies for jobs, not because he or she expects to get a job, but in order to be able to say to others, "I'm still looking. Haven't given up yet."

One day, however, his scene changed. Jesus of Nazareth came to visit the pool and saw him there. This man didn't know who Jesus was, so when Jesus asked him, "Do you want to be made well?" the man answered with what must have been his stock reply. I hear his voice in a kind of whine, as if it were now a computerized answer—push the button of inquiry, and the words come out flat and mechanically: "Sir, I have no one to put me into the pool when the water is stirred up; and while I am making my way, someone else steps down ahead of me" (John 5:7).

I feel the pathos of his answer. But I have to confess that some other feelings also arise in me. And the operative word is, indeed, *confess*, because I don't like my own feelings. I said a moment ago that his answer came in a kind of whine; I suppose that term indicates my perception of this man. I find myself contrasting him with Bartimaeus, the beggar who was blind. When he called to Jesus for healing, Jesus answered, "What do you want me to do for you?" Bartimaeus didn't answer with a report on how long he had been blind, nor with an appeal for sympathy; he simply said, "My teacher, let me see again" (Mark 10:51). When Jesus asks this man at the pool if he wants to be healed, I want him to answer simply, "Yes! For heaven's sake, *yes.*"

Instead, this man tells Jesus why he hasn't already been healed. His answer is part apology, part excuse, and part complaint. When he says that he has no one to help him, I wonder why. Have his friends grown tired of him?

Now, mind you, I'm raising a question about the quality of this man's friends, as well as a question about his personality. Some of our friends aren't as compassionate as they should be. All of us know what it is like, in a time of trouble, to see our friends sort themselves out by their degrees of caring. But some of us have also observed persons who make it very difficult for their friends to remain attentive; perhaps we have even, ourselves, been guilty of such attitudes. How much can friends be expected to endure?

Let me hasten to say that I am drawing my opinion about this man partly from what is revealed a little later in the story. Jesus responds to the man's cautious reply by healing him. Our Lord does so by insisting on the man's own vigorous cooperation: "Stand up, take your mat and walk" (John 5:8). And the man does so, which is surely to his credit. But it is the sabbath, so he is soon confronted by some persons who tell him that he ought not to be working on the sabbath (for even a simple act such as carrying a mat was regarded as work). The man replies that he is carrying the mat because the person who healed him had told him to do so. But he doesn't know Jesus' name.

Soon, however, Jesus seeks him out and gives him a warning: "See, you have been made well! Do not sin any more, so that nothing worse happens to you" (John 5:14). So how does the man respond? He promptly goes to the people who are the potential enemies of his healer and identifies Jesus to them. Surely he couldn't help knowing that he was incriminating Jesus. It was an astonishing act of betrayal. Am I somewhat on target when I wonder if perhaps he had at other times treated friends this way? Was there something in him that made him more anxious to curry favor with power than to be loyal to a benefactor? I don't know. I am only confessing the questions that come to my mind even as I am trying to persuade myself to defend this man.

I think we have to agree that he is not a heroic figure. I contrast him with another man in John's Gospel, a man blind from his birth. When Jesus healed him, people asked his opinion of his healer. The man answered without hesitation, "He is a prophet" (John 9:17). This answer got the man in trouble with the authorities, who pressed him to discredit Jesus in some way. Instead, the man challenged the arrogance of the authorities, and in the end, acknowledged

Jesus as Lord. This is the kind of courage I want to see in the man at the pool. Instead, I see a person who goes out of his way to solicit the favor of those who are in power, and who abruptly denies the one who has healed him. It is very difficult to defend a man like this.

But of course each of us has his or her own personality flaws, and since this person's failings are hard for me to stomach, I need to put forth extra effort to understand him. It's natural to empathize with a person whose failings are like your own. Jesus said that it is quite easy to love those who love us; the test comes when we are asked to love our enemies (Matthew 5:43-48). People with my kind of faults are of course more lovable; they're my kind of people. So when I say of someone's conduct, "I just can't understand how he could do such a thing," the spirit of Jesus answers, "Why don't you give it a try?"

Indeed, Jesus obviously did just that. When the man by the pool answered Jesus' inquiry, "Do you want to be healed?" by a declaration of distress, Jesus did not abandon him or lecture him; he *healed* him. It's very clear that Jesus gave him the benefit of the doubt. And this is grace, isn't it? If Jesus had performed his healings on the basis of some sort of admissions committee, I'm sure this man wouldn't have made it. Someone on the committee (someone like me!) would have said, "He isn't really a prime prospect. He'll flunk out after the first semester." And of course, those doubters would have been right. He did flunk out, hurrying with his newfound powers of locomotion to betray Jesus to the authorities. But I tell you, I'd rather bet with Jesus on people who lose than to reject them and be right.

The world has a fair share of people who seem pro-grammed to lose. If they came to one of our church gatherings where we try to determine spiritual gifts, we'd be hard put to locate their gift—but of course folks like this rarely get that far. We seldom find them in the church, because they hide away on the edge of life, not involving themselves in much of anything. In the most tragic of cases we hear of

them after a violent crime. The neighbors in their apart-
ment complex say, "We never really got to know him. He
seemed like a loner. You couldn't get him to talk to you."
But of course the vast majority of this man's soul mates
don't end up in acts of violence. They just sit by the pool of
life while others are leaping in.

Biblical scholars generally assume that the man by the
pool was a paralytic. What was the paralysis that made him
such a withdrawn soul, or was it the withdrawing that made
him a paralytic? Some say that it is possible for a person to
induce paralysis by a negative state of mind. Might this have
been the man's problem?

In any event, there is surely pathos in this man's statement, "[W]hile I am making my way, someone else steps
down ahead of me" (John 5:7). This was his autobiography
in a sentence. Here is a man who lost every race. If a modern believe-in-yourself religionist had cheerily told him,
"You need a better self-image; think of some time when you
were at your best and form in your mind a picture of yourself as a winner," this poor fellow would have sat there looking at an empty screen.

I've known some people like that. They have been beaten
by life for so long that they become reconciled to it. Don't
tell them that there's a winner deep down inside; they know
better! Sometimes they are persons whose parents didn't
really want them; or who, if they did, didn't know how to
express it. I'm satisfied that there are some families where
defeatism is passed on from generation to generation like a
malignant strain. They are bred to expect the worst. No
wonder they lie by the pool of life without ever finding the
abundant healing that awaits them.

And because they are so self-despising, they encourage
rejection. They come to a setting saying to themselves,
"People here won't like me," and sure enough, we prove
them right. So in time, their only pride is in their defeat.
They rejoice in the size and the scope of it. If they are ill,
they want to tell you, "The doctor says he's never seen an

infection that hung on the way mine has." A person has to have something to glory in!

In the worst scenario (other than the irrational turn to violence), such a person comes to enjoy sitting alone in his or her pain. Drawing down the shades of life, lest some brilliance break in on them, they look for ever darker corners. After all, pain and defeat are the only constants in their lives, the only friends they can count on.

There are moments, of course, in all of our lives when we can empathize with them. Probably all of us have such times; that's why generations have smiled at the song, "Nobody loves me, everybody hates me, guess I'll go eat worms." But most of us don't make a lifetime of such an attitude, and we don't easily sympathize with those who do.

Personally, I've come to feel sorry for this man. I have looked at his case long enough that I'm ready to defend him, though I'm afraid my argument hasn't necessarily impressed you. I see him as possessed by a dreadful, but relatively common, spiritual malignancy; and by God's grace, I intend when I see him to help him. It isn't fun treating such persons. There aren't many spectacular recoveries. Indeed, when recoveries do happen, most people don't realize the extent of the miracle, because the illness is such a subtle thing. It's not as dramatic as deliverance from the drug culture, or a conversion on death row.

But I am awed by my Lord, who stopped one day before the quintessential case of a loser (a man who never won any race), and asked him if he wanted to be healed. And without ever getting the right answer, Jesus nevertheless healed him! In the end, it looks as if Jesus lost on this man, since the man betrayed him. No matter. Our Lord died, not only for those who accept his salvation, but also for those who reject him.

Now that, brothers and sisters, is grace. And as a recipient of God's grace, I not only rejoice in its irrational judgment, I feel compelled to follow its pattern.

CHAPTER 5

A Wild and Wonderful Woman

JOHN 4:7-18, 28-30: A Samaritan woman came to draw water, and Jesus said to her, "Give me a drink." (His disciples had gone to the city to buy food.) The Samaritan woman said to him, "How is it that you, a Jew, ask a drink of me, a woman of Samaria?" (Jews do not share things in common with Samaritans.) Jesus answered her, "If you knew the gift of God, and who it is that is saying to you, 'Give me a drink,' you would have asked him, and he would have given you living water." The woman said to him, "Sir, you have no bucket, and the well is deep. Where do you get that living water? Are you greater than our ancestor Jacob, who gave us the well, and with his sons and his flocks drank from it?" Jesus said to her, "Everyone who drinks of this water will be thirsty again, but those who drink of the water that I will give them will never be thirsty. The water that I will give will become in them a spring of water gushing up to eternal life." The woman said to him, "Sir, give me this water, so that I may never be thirsty or have to keep coming here to draw water."

Jesus said to her, "Go, call your husband, and come back." The woman answered him, "I have no husband." Jesus said to her, "You are right in saying, 'I have no husband'; for you have had five husbands, and the one you have now is not your husband. What you have said is true!" . . . Then the woman left her water jar and went back to the city. She said to the people, "Come and see a man who told me everything I have ever done! He cannot be the Messiah, can he?" They left the city and were on their way to him.

*H*ow do you start a church? At the turn of the twentieth century, as the late William Hyde recalled, it was simple. As a young Methodist preacher, Hyde was taken by train to a small town in Nebraska. He was told that there was one Methodist in the community, but that he had probably become a Presbyterian, that there was a second-floor hall that could no doubt be rented for a gathering place. And then, as the train pulled from the station, the district superintendent called out a simple formula for beginning a church: "Dig or die, Brother Hyde!"

In our day, church planting has become a science. Some progressive seminaries offer special programs, even doctoral studies, in church planting. Statisticians can project how many thousand telephone calls will produce how many hundred in attendance at an opening service, and what mass mailings will appeal to what segments of a population, as well as the type of music, the style of worship, and the level of preaching that will be most effective in a given community.

I confess that I fall somewhere between these two very different methods. The unreconstructed grump in me favors the first, while the researcher in me opts for the second. But of one thing, I am sure. If I were starting a church, I know the person I would want for my first member. I don't know her name, but I know everything else about her, and I can tell you this: Give me this wild and wonderful woman, and with God's help I will soon have a thriving body of believers.

The circumstances of our meeting this woman are not auspicious. It is noontime in the Middle East, a time of day when you don't expect to meet anyone because people, if possible, stay indoors. British playwright Noel Coward said while reflecting on tropical and subtropical climates that "only mad dogs and Englishmen go out in the noonday sun." But this woman is out and about and, furthermore, she is working. Specifically, she is coming to the village well, an empty jar on her head.

In that ancient world, ordinarily it was women who went to the village well for water. It was hard work, but it also had a reward, because the trip offered the opportunity to visit with other women of the village. But the trip to the well was something one did in the cool of the evening, not in the heat of midday. That this woman (I apologize that we have no name for her) was doing the task in midday indicates either that she was a poor household manager, who hadn't rightly calculated her needs for the day, or she was someone who didn't want to be at the well when other women were there. Popular understanding tends to the latter conclusion, since this was a woman who no doubt had a complicated reputation. I think I would also offer another option. Perhaps this was just an extraordinary day, when the family's needs were greater than usual, or some of the precious water was spilled; or perhaps the woman had simply become restless, and wanted to get out of the home for a little while. Yes, I think I will cast a cautious vote for restlessness, because I'm quite sure that this was a restless person. And let me introduce another word too: *providence.* It may be that the circumstances of that morning were providential. Some might say it was luck, some might shrug their shoulders and say, "Things happen"; I dare to venture the prospect of providence. Perhaps grace was at work.

In any event, as the woman approached the well, she saw that someone was there. It was a man, and she was familiar with the ways of men. Soon she could see by his dress that he was a Jewish man, so now she felt quite safe, because she knew a Jewish man would not talk to her. To do so was double jeopardy, since she was both a woman and a Samaritan. But she was barely in position when the stranger asked her for a drink. Rather than answering yes or no, the woman asked how it was that he asked her for a drink, since he was a Jew and she was a woman of Samaria.

We can see the woman more clearly now. It's difficult to guess her age, but we can see that she has lived a lot. Elbert Hubbard, the popular American philosopher from early in the twentieth century, used to say that beauty not only leaves a face with the passage of time, it also leaves behind a record as to where it has gone. She has been a strikingly attractive woman, and although the past tense now seems to apply, nevertheless one can't easily take one's eyes off her.

And so a conversation began to unfold between Jesus of Nazareth and a woman who will always be known to us simply as the Samaritan woman, or the woman at the well. Her quick rejoinder to Jesus' question showed that she was someone who knew how to take care of herself; today we would call her "street smart." She wasn't really afraid of anyone; one judges that she had come this far by her wits, and that she was ready to continue by the same method.

I suppose everyone has a secret; most of us have several. Jesus unearths this woman's secret when he asks her to bring her husband, and she replies that she doesn't have one, at which point Jesus notes, perhaps sardonically, that her answer is true: She's had five, and the man with whom she is now living isn't her husband.

What shall we make of such a story? Was this woman the tabloid material of Samaria? Or was she, perhaps, the kind of person who insisted on making the same kind of mistake again and again, so that she always married the kind of man with whom matrimonial success was impossible? Did she solicit defeat and pain? Some people seem to, you know. Or could it be that she was unable to conceive, and that in a world where a woman was supposed to produce children, men—who could divorce easily in that first-century world— simply disposed of her when she didn't do what they reasoned she was supposed to do?

Whatever the cause of her checkered marital record, this experience must have been the determining issue of her life. A short while later, when she told her friends about Jesus, her story was brief: "Come and see a man who told me everything I have ever done!" (John 4:29). In truth, Jesus had spoken about only one element in her life, but it was the element that seemed to her to characterize all that she was.

We're like that, you know. We let some major, decimating factor come into life, and we allow it to define us. A man who had been divorced said, "I feel like I'm wearing a big 'D' on my coat. That's who I am: Divorced." A woman with a malignancy told me, "I can't help feeling that people know me now by just one fact, that I have cancer. I hate it that I have made this sickness the boundaries of my personality, but I can't seem to help it." I venture this was the mood of the woman of Samaria. One could have said a score of important things about her life, her character, her personality, but it seemed to her that everything about herself could be summarized in six words: five husbands and a live-in man. So she said of Jesus, "He told me everything I have ever done."

Well, I can tell you more about her. She was, in the truest sense of the word, a religious seeker. The moment Jesus referred to her distressed personal life, she identified him as a prophet and addressed him with what was the most important religious question in her life. She was a Samaritan woman and Jesus was a Jew—which means that they were half-siblings, so to speak—and she knew that a few major religious differences separated them, even though they were both descendants of Jacob.

The biggest issue was the place of worship. For centuries, Jerusalem had been the site of the temple and the place to which devout Jews traveled at least once a year for one of their major religious festivals. But after the division between the northern and the southern tribes, the people in the north had worshiped at a mountain in Samaria—and it was to these northern people and their beliefs that the woman of Samaria belonged.

So when she said to Jesus, "Our ancestors worshiped on this mountain, but you say that the place where people must worship is in Jerusalem" (John 4:20), she was not raising some peculiar doctrinal issue. In truth, she was asking the granddaddy of all questions, the ultimate issue of life: "How and where do I find God?"

Nor is it surprising, then, that after Jesus had answered this question the woman moved to a subject just one step removed from the ultimate question: the coming of the Messiah, or the Christ. Jews and Samaritans understood that with the coming of the Messiah, all of the purposes of God would at last be fulfilled, so this remarkable woman was following a logical line in her dialogue.

And was it possible too that she was seeing something more, something special, in her unknown companion? Could it be that although she had perceived him to be a prophet, she now was wondering if he might be more? Was there some wistfulness in her statement, "I know that Messiah is coming" (John 4:25), with perhaps a longing that this stranger, this Jew who had broken so many barriers to talk with her, and who by doing so had already lifted her status in ways beyond her imagining—could it be that *he* might be the Messiah?

Whatever her longings may or may not have been, Jesus answered directly and surely, "I am he, the one who is speaking to you" (John 4:26). In a conversation that up to that point had so often been couched in figurative and metaphorical language, suddenly there was an utterly unequivocal statement: *I am he.* This is all the more remarkable when one recalls that when Simon Peter identified Jesus as the Messiah, Jesus "sternly ordered the disciples not to tell anyone that he was the Messiah" (Matthew 16:20). How strange and how gracious that Jesus would be so completely candid with this woman!

At this moment, the disciples reappeared on the scene, and although they were "astonished" to find him talking with a woman, no one dared to say so. The woman, meanwhile, is captured by an ultimate urgency. She leaves behind the water jar that had been her reason, earlier in the day, for making this trip, and hurries back to her city with the key word of the evangelist: *Come.* "Come and see a man who told me everything I have ever done! He cannot be the Messiah, can he?" (John 4:29).

What follows is without parallel in the four Gospels. "Many Samaritans from that city" believed in Jesus because of the woman's testimony—the testimony of how Jesus had searched her heart ("He told me everything I have ever done"). When these folk saw Jesus for themselves, they asked him to stay with them, and he stayed two days. This is the only instance recorded in the Gospels where Jesus extended his residency in a community at the request of the inhabitants—and it happened, of course, in the most unlikely of places, a town in Samaria, the region Jews avoided. "[M]any more" then believed; and in explaining their believing, they paid the woman an unwitting compliment: "It is no longer because of what you said that we believe, for we have heard for ourselves, and we know that this is truly the Savior of the world" (John 4:42).

Their language is significant. They identify Jesus not simply as a prophet, nor even as the Messiah, but as "the Savior of the world." Did Jesus tell these people of Samaria some things about himself that he didn't commonly say to the crowds? And of course we pause at the words "of the world." The Samaritans, so accustomed to being despised, have been introduced to one who embraces not only the Jews, but also Samaritans; and if you can leap that formidable boundary, it's easy to imagine embracing the whole world.

We don't know how many persons in that Samaritan city were converted, but it was obviously a substantial number. Indeed, it seems clear that more people in that city accepted Jesus as Messiah and Lord than in any other community prior to our Lord's crucifixion and resurrection. And it all began with this woman who had come to the well in midday to get water.

You may not like my identifying her by the adjective *wild*. But wouldn't we use that adjective, or some close synonym, to describe such a person today? If your conversation turned to someone who had been married five times and who now was living with someone out of wedlock, someone in the circle would surely say, "She's a wild one, isn't she!" And yet it was this unlikely woman who started the church in Sychar, Samaria.

I think she's wonderful, and if I were going to start a church, I'd like for her to be my first member. True, her personal record leaves something to be desired. Some would call her a longtime loser, but from a strictly theological point of view, we're all longtime losers; we're all in need of God's grace. And the truth is, she must also have been a longtime seeker, else she wouldn't have engaged so readily and so appropriately in the conversation that led to her recognizing Jesus as the Christ.

I'm impressed, too, that the people of her village were convinced by her witness. Some of us excuse ourselves from sharing our faith story because we think people might not believe us. This Samaritan woman ought to dispel any such argument; if *she* could make a case for faith, then almost *anyone* could. I expect that the persuasiveness of her presentation came in the simple integrity of it. Her old friends (and enemies) could see that her encounter with Jesus had come through to her in some dramatic way, and they couldn't help wanting to see what this strange Jew, who had so changed her, might do for them. I wish I could have seen her countenance when she returned to Sychar, after her visit with Jesus; I'm sure I would have been persuaded too.

Well, that's my formula for starting a church. Perhaps it isn't much of an improvement on "Dig or die, Brother Hyde," and it surely doesn't compare with the contemporary approach that is built on a mountain of statistics and surveys. And yet, I'm confident that my method will work. Give me some wild and wonderful woman—or, for that matter, a wild and wonderful man—who has come to know a transforming meeting with Jesus the Christ, and we will soon have a church. A great, warm, wonderful church. The formula is as old as the Gospel of John.

CHAPTER 6

The Importance of Being Bilingual

MARK 10:46-52: They came to Jericho. As he and his disciples and a large crowd were leaving Jericho, Bartimaeus son of Timaeus, a blind beggar, was sitting by the roadside. When he heard that it was Jesus of Nazareth, he began to shout out and say, "Jesus, Son of David, have mercy on me!" Many sternly ordered him to be quiet, but he cried out even more loudly, "Son of David, have mercy on me!" Jesus stood still and said, "Call him here." And they called the blind man, saying to him, "Take heart; get up, he is calling you." So throwing off his cloak, he sprang up and came to Jesus. Then Jesus said to him, "What do you want me to do for you?" The blind man said to him, "My teacher, let me see again." Jesus said to him, "Go; your faith has made you well." Immediately he regained his sight and followed him on the way.

*M*y daughter is a French professor. I say this not only with fatherly pride, but also with amazement. Yes, and with embarrassment, too. Because, you see, the only language I speak is English. Mind you, I've studied Latin, Greek, and German, but English is the only language I speak.

And yes, I know the old joke: "What do you call someone who speaks two languages?"

"Bilingual."

"And what do you call someone who speaks only one language?"

"An American."

Yes, I know that. But I like to make a mild defense for us Americans. We can travel hundreds and hundreds of miles and need to speak only English, while a European makes a trip the equivalent of Indiana to Iowa and needs another language if he or she is to manage life halfway successfully.

That's why a long-ago beggar named Bartimaeus is one of my very special heroes. He was intelligent enough to know that he needed to be bilingual in order to manage life. And one day he did so with a grand flourish.

This is remarkable, because from most vantage points, Bartimaeus didn't have much going for him. Even his name was something of a putdown. It means "son of Timaeus," which was really a secondary classification in his world—a last name, really, as in "Simon, son of John," or "David, son of Jesse." This was the way you distinguished a person from all of the other people who had the same given name. But in the case of Bartimaeus, it appears that somehow his given name had been lost. He was commonly known simply as "the son of Timaeus." Whatever his first name may have been, we don't really know.

Everything else about him was equally limited. As I said a moment ago, he was a beggar. He was also blind. In a culture that made no provision for persons with disabilities, he was doing the only thing he was able to do—beg.

Most of us are so powerfully shaped by our circumstances, and by what others tell us we are. One needs great inner strength to be poor and deprived, and yet not look down on oneself; or to be told, day after day, that you're useless and a burden on society, and yet think of yourself as having some worth; or to be scorned and pushed aside, yet see yourself as having a right to live. I cannot imagine what it would be like to step out into the darkness every day to grope my way to a begging post, knowing that all day long I would suffer rejection and contempt. But this is the only world, the only way of life, that the son of Timaeus knew. And it was the only life he could ever expect to know.

But Bartimaeus was bilingual! This was his wonderful, hidden strength. I don't know that anyone knew it, or that anyone cared. After all, most people thought his only vocabulary was four or five words of crude Aramaic: "Alms, sir! Can you help a beggar?" Passersby didn't know that he had a second language, and they surely didn't know that one day he would use that second language with such effectiveness that his life would be transformed; or that, come to think of it, we would be talking or writing about him two thousand years later.

Here's the way it happened. Bartimaeus was heading out one day to one of his usual begging places, probably on the road leading out of Jericho toward Jerusalem. It was usually a well-traveled road, but today Bartimaeus noticed a bustle of unusual excitement. His well-honed senses—the senses that had helped him to survive in a disadvantaged world— told him that the crowd was not only exceptionally large, but that it also possessed a peculiar kind of awed stillness. Jesus of Nazareth, someone said, was passing by.

That's all Bartimaeus needed to know. As I've said, he was a bilingualist, and this was an occasion that called for his second language. And he employed it with all of his might. He ventured no tentative, uncertain call, but an insistent shout: "Jesus, Son of David, have mercy on me!" (Mark 10:47). At first it looked as if his effort would fail. A great many people in the crowd "sternly ordered him to be quiet" (Mark 10:48). He was intruding on the crowd's opportunity to listen to the popular itinerant teacher. They would have resented such a discourtesy from almost anyone, but it was unthinkable from this beggar. Observers must have felt that it was audacious for someone of Bartimaeus's ilk to expect special attention from anyone. Besides, since they didn't recognize the language in which Bartimaeus was speaking, I suspect they reasoned simply that the man was doing his usual thing, begging for alms.

But Bartimaeus wasn't about to be shut down. He called out again, now more loudly than before, "Jesus, Son of

David, have mercy on me!" He had both eloquence and insistence in this second tongue. It seems, too, that he knew something many in the crowd didn't know; or if they knew it, they were unduly cautious about saying it. Most of them would have addressed Jesus as "Jesus of Nazareth," but Bartimaeus called him "Jesus, *Son of David.*" For some quite remarkable reason, Bartimaeus was tracing Jesus back to his key ancestor, King David.

Now this is surprising, and I think the Gospel writer intends for us to see that it is so. He has just told us that Bartimaeus has learned "that it was Jesus of Nazareth" who was passing by. Bartimaeus doesn't address him as Jesus of Nazareth, however; he calls him "Jesus, Son of David." In doing so, Bartimaeus was making a confession of faith. He was saying, in faith shorthand, that Jesus was the Messiah, and that he was calling upon him as such. His appeal to Jesus was not an appeal to a popular teacher, or even to a noted, dynamic healer. Bartimaeus was appealing on the grounds that Jesus was the Christ of God, the one who according to the prophets was to come from the line of David.

At this moment, another voice cut through the street sounds. It was Jesus, saying simply, "Call him here" (Mark 10:49). The people who a few moments before had been trying to silence Bartimaeus now became solicitous. "Lucky fellow," they said. "Hurry! He's calling you." The beggar needed no further prodding. He threw off his poor beggar cloak and fumbled his way to Jesus, helped along no doubt by now-sympathetic bystanders. Jesus asked him what he wanted, and Bartimaeus wasted no time in framing his answer. "My teacher," he said, "let me see again" (Mark 10:51). Jesus was just as quick in answering. "Go; your faith has made you well" (Mark 10:52). And just that quickly, the blind man received his sight and followed Jesus on the way.

However you look at it, this is a remarkable story. Many of us, as believers, read it as the story of a miracle: a blind man who called out to Jesus Christ and received his sight. On the other hand, a doubter may see it only as part of the folklore of the church; he doesn't necessarily believe it, but he thinks it is beautiful for its depiction of human longing.

But I would like for you to see it as the story of a person who was bilingual, and who used his talent in a powerful way. I don't know how well he did in his second language, which was probably Aramaic. His vocabulary may have been very sparse; after all, as I indicated earlier, you don't need to know many words in order to make a living by begging. But in his primary language, which was *prayer*, he was eloquent in the extreme. So eloquent, in fact, that he caused the Messiah, and all of heaven, to stop; and he was healed. And the secret, the whole wonderful secret, is in his being bilingual. He knew the language of his country, Aramaic, and he knew the language of heaven, which is prayer.

Perhaps you noticed a moment ago how I described those two languages. I referred to Aramaic as Bartimaeus's second language, and prayer as his primary language. Because whatever language you most commonly speak (English, for me), it is, in a very special sense, your second language. Your primary language, the one you first knew, was prayer.

That's because we human beings are praying creatures. Prayer comes naturally to us, because the breath of God is in us. The deep that is in us, the most profound reality of who we are, is the divine. To pray is to return to our native tongue.

But as we live out our lives, most of us lose touch with our native language. I knew a man who spoke nothing but German for the first six years of his life. But then he entered school and began to speak English, and from that time forward he spoke English almost exclusively. By the time that I knew him, when he was a man in his fifties, he didn't understand any German. He recognized a few words here and there, but he had lost touch with his earthly native tongue.

That's what has happened to a great many of us human beings as regards prayer. As children, we once understood

the language of heaven. Prayer came easily to us—
unaffected, natural, simple, and direct. It was so direct, in
fact, that adults often found it amusing, until of course they
convinced us to make prayer special, ritualistic, and unnatu-
ral. Then, too, as the years go by, almost the only language
we hear, day after day, is earthly and secular. It's the language of buying and selling, of getting and accumulating, of
the here and now. Mind you, it is necessary language. I bear
no case against it as such; indeed, I have tried through most
of my life to master its usage. We need a certain amount of
it simply to carry on our daily lives, because it is the medi-
um of intellectual and social exchange in the world in
which we live.

But if, as the years go by, this is the only language we
know, we become less than human. I must be very emphatic
about this. If you or I become fluent in a dozen earthly
tongues—from English to Urdu—and if we can read ten
more—including ancient Sanskrit—but we no longer speak
the language of prayer, then we are poor, one-language persons, and our lives are desperately limited.

And we have a problem. If a person could really, fully do
business on this earth speaking only the languages of earth,
perhaps the primary tongue wouldn't matter so much. But
you and I are, by nature, citizens of two worlds, the earthly
and the spiritual. And if we can't converse in the spiritual—
if we are bumbling souls when it comes to the language of
prayer—then we aren't really equipped to live as God
meant us to live.

But at this moment, I think I hear someone raising a
question about my hero of this Scripture, Bartimaeus. What
was so eloquent about his prayer, you ask. All he said was,
"Jesus, Son of David, have mercy on me"; and then, in
answer to Jesus' question, "My teacher, let me see again."
What is so remarkable about that?

For one thing, that Bartimaeus knew who Jesus was. I
have no idea how he sensed that he should address Jesus as
"the Son of David," which was a messianic term. Perhaps

Bartimaeus was one of those country-store theologians whom our world has known in every generation, and who can be found in virtually every town. This is the kind of person who has somehow, out of simple earnestness, come to know far more than might be expected. Whatever the background of Bartimaeus's knowledge, he addressed Jesus as only a person of spiritual insight would have thought or dared to do.

Then, too, Bartimaeus had faith. He had faith enough to ask, then the faith to keep on asking when everyone was trying to silence him. Still more, after he was healed, he chose to follow Jesus along the way. Most of the persons whom Jesus healed, or for whom he worked miracles, simply went on their way, pursuing the life they had previously known. Some didn't even bother to say thank you. But this man, more fluent in the language of heaven, intended to follow Jesus. He wanted more than the healing of his blindness. This was a man who was fluent in his native tongue, prayer.

Why was this so? What made Bartimaeus a person of holy fluency? In truth, he had no advantages over you and me. Except, perhaps, one: He had the advantage of a passionate need. When it comes to prayer, despair makes one eloquent. And in this respect, his poverty was a consequential asset. He was so poor that he wasn't distracted by other possible solutions to his problem. Sometimes our prayers lack eloquence because prayer seems to us, in truth, to be rather incidental, or perhaps a kind of convenience. After all, if prayer doesn't work we can always invest more of our hopes in those remedies that money can buy, or that logic can contrive. I hate to say it, but our comparative abundance may get in the way of greater skill in our native tongue, prayer. Mind you, despair and faith are not the same, but sometimes despair impels our search for faith.

I want so much for you and me to understand the importance of being bilingual. I want us to realize that a person who can talk only in the dialects of business, sports, sex, literature, philosophy, and the news of the day is fatally disadvantaged. Because you and I must eventually, some day, do business with God—in this world, and in the world to come. How pathetic to think that we might have to stand before God, eloquent in business, sports, and gossip, and babbling like an infant when it comes to the divine tongue!

Here's the good news. Divine eloquence is within every person's reach, because it involves the language all of us are equipped to speak. But—as with any other language—you have to care enough to spend some time learning the fundamentals of the language and then expanding your vocabulary and your ease of expression.

Now is the time to be at it. Not when you're facing surgery the next day, or when your family is falling apart, and certainly not when you're dying. Now is the time, the ideal time, to become eloquent in our native tongue. *Prayer*—the language that works in both time and eternity.

CHAPTER 7

Expecting a Little King

MARK 11:1-10: When they were approaching Jerusalem, at Bethphage and Bethany, near the Mount of Olives, he sent two of his disciples and said to them, "Go into the village ahead of you, and immediately as you enter it, you will find tied there a colt that has never been ridden; untie it and bring it. If anyone says to you, 'Why are you doing this?' just say this, 'The Lord needs it and will send it back here immediately.'" They went away and found a colt tied near a door, outside in the street. As they were untying it, some of the bystanders said to them, "What are you doing, untying the colt?" They told them what Jesus had said; and they allowed them to take it. Then they brought the colt to Jesus and threw their cloaks on it; and he sat on it. Many people spread their cloaks on the road, and others spread leafy branches that they had cut in the fields. Then those who went ahead and those who followed were shouting,

"Hosanna!
Blessed is the one who comes
in the name of the Lord!
Blessed is the coming king-
dom of our ancestor
David!
Hosanna in the highest heaven!"

I love Palm Sunday. It's one of my favorite days. If those wonderful people at Hallmark or American Greetings ever figure out a way to merchandise it, Palm Sunday may catch on in a big way. I can imagine chocolate donkeys, cards in the shape of palm leaves, and recordings of little children singing Hosanna.

I love Palm Sunday because of a store of childhood

memories. Palm Sunday seemed in those long-ago times to be a day that belonged in a special way to children. After all, the hymn that we usually sang on that day featured children:

> Into the city I'd follow the children's band,
>   waving a branch of the palm tree high in my hand;
> one of his heralds, yes, I would sing
>   loudest hosannas, "Jesus is King!"

(WILLIAM H. PARKER, "TELL ME THE STORIES OF JESUS," 1855)

I'm sure I've carried something of that idyllic picture into my adult perception of Palm Sunday, and probably my adult understanding has reinforced it. As an adult I enter Palm Sunday with a realization that I am entering Holy Week, and that before I reach Easter I will pass through the heavy solemnity of Maundy Thursday, the exquisite darkness of Good Friday, and the silence of Saturday. I seem to take special hold of Palm Sunday, as if acknowledging that its festive sense of victory is soon to be put to the test.

And I love Palm Sunday because of the beautiful faith of Jesus' followers. One wonders why the people were so captured by Jesus' entry into Jerusalem. He had chosen a most unlikely venue. No beast of burden was more common to the culture, and less possessed of glamor, than the donkey. The sight of one still evokes a kind of affectionate laughter. And Jesus chose not simply a donkey, but a colt that had never been ridden; what might one expect of such a creature as this?

We are sometimes reminded that in ancient times the donkey was a symbol of peace. It was hardly, however, a creature of majesty. Indeed, it seems difficult to take seriously someone who makes an entrance on such a ridiculous little creature. And yet, the crowds applauded Jesus. Some people took off their cloaks (this in a world where the poor generally had only one outer garment) and spread them in the pathway of the animal and its rider. Still others ran to nearby fields and cut branches and leaves to pave the path.

And then, as if they had lost all sense of reality, they began to call, "Hosanna!" Twenty centuries later, we see nothing but religious meaning in that word. But in the first-century world, the word was full of political significance, and it was religious at that point where religious faith coincided with political dreams. It meant, literally, "save now," and it was the term an oppressed people would use in calling for help from a conqueror.

And it's clear enough that this was what the shouters had in mind. They were caught up in the kind of chant that our generation most often hears at a sporting event, but that can still electrify a crowd with political excitement. One can easily imagine the kind of sing-song excitement that began to rock the crowd:

> "Hosanna!
> Blessed is the one who comes
> in the name of the Lord!
> Blessed is the coming kingdom
> of our ancestor David!
> Hosanna in the highest heaven!"
> (MARK 11:9-10)

But even as I am taken by the enthusiasm of the crowd, the sensible part of me is bemused. By what logic could they have become so ecstatic? A solitary figure on a funny little donkey colt could hardly give a person reason to think the political scene was going to change! There was no army in his wake, and as for the little company of his closest followers—those constituting the inner circle that would conceivably become Jesus' cabinet—they were a rather motley group of fishermen and small-business people. As far as anyone could see, there wasn't a charismatic leader in the whole group.

Besides, Jesus himself hadn't given any evidence of political ambition. He had healed the sick, but that didn't give him potential political clout. True, he often used a quasi-political term, "the kingdom of heaven," or "the kingdom of

God." But when he told people what he meant by the term, he used enigmatic language that could hardly be expected to focus their political enthusiasm. The kingdom of God, he said, was like a grain of mustard seed; or again, it was like leaven that a housewife might put into a lump of dough. What kind of political incitement is that?

So we're left wondering why the people got so excited as to pave Jesus' way with coats and leaves, and to shout out their dreams. Perhaps they were simply so hungry for a leader that almost *anyone* would give rise to their dreams. And yet, their cries and deeds were no empty game. Some Pharisees—easily the single most powerful group in Israel—spoke their angry resentment at the ardor of the crowds (Luke 19:39). Poor folk didn't want to be on the wrong side of people like the Pharisees, so it's remarkable that the people hailing Jesus would take a chance on incurring the disfavor of the Pharisees.

So I marvel at the simple folk who hailed Jesus as their potential deliverer. I wonder how they could see so much in this man on a donkey's colt. Mind you, we have to try to get into the mind-set of that first-century world, which is hard to do when we know nineteen centuries and more of the sequel. But if we make such an adjustment, we can't help wondering how they could be caught up in such irrational hope.

And yet, with all of that, I have to tell you that the adoring crowds saw so little, so very little. They called Jesus the leader of the coming kingdom. But they were looking for a little king. Their expectations were far too small.

They saw someone, for instance, who would deliver them from the power of the Roman Empire. At first glance, that seems like miracle enough. The reach of the Roman Empire, and its precision-efficiency, made the nation of Israel seem absurd by comparison. I'm sure that the average first-century Jew envisioned, at best, a period that might compare with the forty golden years of their beloved King David. It had been more than eight centuries since they had known such security, because even the best of the interven-ing kings had lived in peril of the nations around them, or with uneasy compromise.

But this dream of freedom from the Roman Empire, extravagant as it might have seemed to the crowds cheering by the roadside, was a little dream for a little king. Jesus Christ had come to be the king not only for Israel, but for all of humankind; and his reign, not for forty years and not even for a continuing dynasty, but for eternity.

The adoring crowds could hardly have grasped such an idea. They saw a little king because they were working from the limits of their experience and their history. We're all like that. We fence God in by the boundaries of our experi-ence. "How much do Daddy and Mommy love you?" we ask a three-year-old; and the child stretches baby arms to their limit while answering happily, "This much!" Yes, indeed— and vastly more. But a child's capacity to perceive and to describe is limited by the length of his arms and the meas-ure of his experience.

So it is with our expectations when we acknowledge Jesus Christ as Lord of our lives. After all, we have so little basis for comparison. Our secular culture promises extravagant possibilities from miracle drugs, or from investments, or from the lottery genie that may drive to our address. We evaluate such problems cautiously, as we should; and then we recognize, with pain, that we need much more than that, and we want much more. Something deep within insists that life ought to hold more. But we rarely realize that the "much more," the overflowing life we desire, awaits us in Jesus Christ. We think he is a membership to be joined, a cause to which we enlist, a doctrine to which we will sub-scribe. We are slow to understand that he is a King in whom all of life finds a new center and a new circumference, new time and new eternity.

When I became a Christian, as a boy of not yet eleven, it was a kind of Palm Sunday for me. I sensed, in a very real way, that I had entered a new relationship with God. If palm branches had been available in Iowa that autumn evening, I would have looked for a place to spread them. But wonderful as that moment was, and as deeply as I felt it, I had no idea of all that was to follow. Jesus was now my king, but I had no idea of the extent or the wonder of his kingdom. I knew nothing of the increasing beauty I would find in the Bible in the years that followed, nor of the comfort and strength that would come my way in future years of difficult passages. And I surely had no idea of the joy of the daily faith-walk I would come, through the years, to know.

Nor did I know the full price of membership in Christ's kingdom. A few years later I came to know a wonderful, gentle man from Indiana. Barty told me, during several earnest conversations, "If I had known, when I was saved, all that Christ would eventually expect of me, I would never have begun the journey. But I have come into my Lord's demands progressively. I can handle now what would have been beyond me when I started." I know, in my own fashion, what Barty meant.

So I wonder about the crowds that called Hosanna that day. In the intoxicating ecstasy of that moment, they couldn't have imagined that before the week was out this wondrous figure would be publicly humiliated, decried, abused, and crucified. I expect that it is possible that some who hailed Jesus on Sunday called for his crucifixion on Friday, or at the least, were silent while others made such a call. But on Palm Sunday, when they rejoiced in Jesus' coming kingdom, they had no idea of the price of that kingdom. They were looking for a small king, a comfortable one, a convenient one. But while Jesus comforts, he is not comfortable, and while he is near for our call, he is not convenient. He is Lord of all, or nothing at all. A king of such magnitude is a king of ultimate demands. Jesus is not a little king, either in his power or in his commands.

But consider the gentle strength of Jesus. Seeing the rather naive expectations of his followers on the first Palm Sunday, he did not reject them for their limited vision, nor did he belittle them. At our safe distance of twenty centuries, we can be amused that they had such limited understanding of our Lord. But Jesus accepted their worship as a sincere expression of their love.

And so he does still. We rarely think, in our moments of earnest worship, of the larger demands of our faith. We sing, in the grand words of Frances Havergal, "Take my silver and my gold; / not a mite would I withhold" ("Take My Life and Let It Be"), but only the tune remains when we determine how much of our income will be given to God and to human need. I find it relatively easy to embrace the whole world with a generality of love, but I find it hard to apply that love to some specific individuals. My palm branches are so often pleasant, well-meaning, and terribly shallow. Without realizing it, I like to keep my king small and manageable. And of course, a manageable king is a contradiction in terms.

I expect that we American believers are especially susceptible to a Palm Sunday syndrome. By what appears to be our good fortune, we know much more about Palm Sunday than about Gethsemane or Calvary. Believers in so many parts of the world declare their faith at the peril of their lives. Even when we are in our most compassionate mood, their sufferings seem remote and unreal. Our usual perception of the Kingship of Jesus seldom contemplates the possibility of serious persecution, let alone martyrdom. Consciously or not, we choose a little king.

I don't think our Lord condemns us for our limited vision, just as he did not reject his supporters on that first Palm Sunday. But he cherishes a greater vision for us, and we ought to seek such a vision too. I expect that we're not fully capable of seeing the true grandeur of our Lord, but it is a vision we can grow into. And it is one we ought to seek. Because the more surely we see the greatness of our King, the more we will fulfill our ordained potential as his subjects.

A generation and more after the first Palm Sunday, a man

in exile on the Isle of Patmos envisioned another day of palm branches. The day he perceived has not yet been fulfilled, but it is coming, no doubt about it. His vision was of no little king and no little kingdom. He saw "a great multitude that no one could count, from every nation, from all tribes and peoples and languages, standing before the throne and before the Lamb, robed in white, with palm branches in their hands" (Revelation 7:9).

A new Palm Sunday! And the cry of this vast multitude is strangely reminiscent of the first Palm Sunday. Long ago they cried, "Hosanna! Save now!" The coming multitude sings of salvation completed:

> "Salvation belongs to our God
>   who is seated on the throne,
>   and to the Lamb!"
> (REVELATION 7:10)

The long-ago crowd (did they number in the scores, or perhaps a few hundred?) hoped for a little king. A multitude beyond numbering, in a day still to come, hails the eternal ruler. In the first century, they hailed what they believed would be God's saving action; in another day, the writer of Revelation tells us, there will be a celebration of a victory fully won.

That first Palm Sunday throng were expecting a little king. But don't smile on them indulgently. Whatever the limits of their vision, it was focused on the right person. In truth, it is because of their faith, and that of millions since then with similar limited vision, that there will someday be such a multitude for the climaxing celebration.

Even at my best, my faith is in the "little king" category. Yours too? If so, let us rejoice that we are part of an eventually triumphant multitude. It is from our little visions that God is making the ultimate victory.

CHAPTER 8

Once There Was a Table

LUKE 22:7-23: Then came the day of Unleavened Bread, on which the Passover lamb had to be sacrificed. So Jesus sent Peter and John, saying, "Go and prepare the Passover meal for us that we may eat it." They asked him, "Where do you want us to make preparations for it?" "Listen," he said to them, "when you have entered the city, a man carrying a jar of water will meet you; follow him into the house he enters and say to the owner of the house, 'The teacher asks you, "Where is the guest room, where I may eat the Passover with my disciples?"' He will show you a large room upstairs, already furnished. Make preparations for us there." So they went and found everything as he had told them; and they prepared the Passover meal.

When the hour came, he took his place at the table, and the apostles with him. He said to them, "I have eagerly desired to eat this Passover with you before I suffer; for I tell you, I will not eat it until it is fulfilled in the kingdom of God." Then he took a cup, and after giving thanks he said, "Take this and divide it among yourselves; for I tell you that from now on I will not drink of the fruit of the vine until the kingdom of God comes." Then he took a loaf of bread, and when he had given thanks, he broke it and gave it to them, saying, "This is my body, which is given for you. Do this in remembrance of me." And he did the same with the cup after supper, saying, "This cup that is poured out for you is the new covenant in my blood. But see, the one who betrays me is with me, and his hand is on the table. For the Son of Man is going as it has been determined, but woe to that one by whom he is betrayed!" Then they began to ask one another, which one of them it could be who would do this.

Atable is such a common article that we pretty much take it for granted. I have concluded, however, that the table is probably humanity's first civilizing piece of furniture. Beds and chairs are essential for comfort; they have a basic utilitarian function. One doesn't need any philosophical basis for fashioning a place to sit or lie down. But a table civilizes. After all, you can eat standing up, or even on the run. Indeed, a good many people do so these days, which may be evidence that we are beginning to regress. But when you sit at a table, you confess, know it or not, that eating is something more than simply stoking some internal furnace or putting fuel in some gastronomic tank.

At its best, a table transforms a meal into a social occasion, whether with friends or family or business associates. Perhaps that's why, when we're eating alone, some of us read a book, a magazine, or a newspaper, or even watch a television screen, because such items provide ersatz company. A table, I repeat, is a socializing, civilizing piece of furniture—probably the first unnecessary item we humans invented. And perhaps in our world of fast food, junk food, microwaves, and breakfast bars, the decline of the table may be one of the significant evidences of the decline of civilized living.

I wonder when tables first became part of our human experience? When did we lift eating to an event, rather than simply a necessity? And isn't it interesting how some of us— actually, how women—will make a table when none exists? You go on a picnic, expecting to eat on the ground, and a woman quickly pulls a tablecloth of some sort out of a basket and spreads it across the grass. Without a doubt it was a woman who invented the first table. Someplace where there was only a mat on which to sleep, and crude chairs for sitting, a woman must have said, "We need a place to eat." Her husband no doubt said, "Hands will do." "For a savage like you," the woman answered. "But our children are going to be civilized. Now, you get a good slab of wood, and put four legs under it, and we'll call it a table. Next week, I plan to invent napkins."

Have you considered how important tables were in the life of Jesus? It is clear that one of the places Jesus loved most was the table of Mary, Martha, and Lazarus. Yes, this was the home where the two sisters were set at odds about a meal preparation. But come to think of it, even that fretting was a kind of tribute to the importance of the social experience of gathering around a table; Martha wanted everything to be just right because a table deserves it. This is also the home where Jesus went during the last week of his life, because at this table of hospitality he obviously found restoration.

And do you remember that it was when Jesus was eating with a Pharisee that a notorious sinful woman interrupted the occasion by pouring perfume on his feet, mixed with her tears? It happened at a table.

On another occasion, a table is implied. A Canaanite woman followed Jesus and his disciples, asking that her daughter be healed. Jesus answered in a way that, from a distance, seems brusque. It isn't right, he explained, to take the children's food and toss it to the dogs. "Yes, Lord," the woman answered, "yet even the dogs eat the crumbs that fall from their masters' table" (*see* Matthew 15:21-28). And Jesus granted the request of this woman who, in faith, had the nimbleness of mind to pick up Jesus' analogy of a table and turn it to her own loving purposes.

And so it is, all through the four Gospels. So many of Jesus' most notable encounters came at one table or another.

But nothing, however, like that special table that we now refer to as *the table of the Lord*. On a night only a few hours before Jesus was brought to trial, beaten, and then crucified, he put a whole new meaning into the very word *table*. Artists over the centuries and around the world have invested their best talent to draw that table and its gathered guests.

The gathering didn't start with much promise. Peter and John had found a large, second-story room where the group would be able to meet. They had come together in the fashion of men: a bit noisy, joshing with one another, talking about the events of the day. Eventually they found their places at the table. In those days people didn't sit around a table, as we do; they reclined. This was a symbol of persons who were free and who could eat with comfort; slaves might have to eat standing, but free persons reclined in casual dignity. It was also a sign of unhurried eating, with easy conversation.

So what did they talk about? The Bible is a disarmingly honest book. As the disciples sat at the table, in the hours before Jesus was crucified, they argued about "which one of them was to be regarded as the greatest" (Luke 22:24). It wasn't a very noble conversation! As a matter of fact, it was downright petty. Now we might excuse them in a measure by saying that they didn't realize the gravity of the hour and the nearness of their Lord's suffering. But of course, that's the point: They were so self-absorbed in their dreams of greatness that they didn't sense Jesus' pain. Self-centeredness does its greatest harm not in intentional acts of evil, but in neglect and insensitivity. So Jesus talked with them about what constitutes true greatness. If you want to be great, he said, you will need to serve. Service is the measure of greatness.

Then there was more conversation, and food—the special food of the Passover meal. But the part of the meal that matters most to us was a brief ceremony that occurred in the course of the meal. In a way, it might at the time have seemed almost incidental. In fact, it's surprising that those who were present remembered it, because it could so easily have been lost in the variety of things that happened that night. Jesus didn't say, "Now here is a special ceremony that I want you to remember." Rather, he seemed to weave the two high moments into the meal almost casually. Count it something of a divine miracle that the disciples preserved it.

Because, you see, it happened like this. While they were passing the food and drink, Jesus took bread, gave thanks over it, broke it, and gave some to the disciples. But as he did so, he said a peculiar thing: "This is my body, which is given for you. Do this in remembrance of me" (Luke 22:19). Do *what* in remembrance of him? Eat the bread! "It's my body," he said. "I'm giving it for you. Eat it."

What a peculiar statement, and what a strange request! I wonder if they looked at one another with a slight lift of the eyebrows. Jesus often said things that perplexed them, but this was a bit much. His body? This bread, his body? Did Thomas, perhaps, break off his piece and mutter to the person next to him, "Doesn't look like a body to me. Just bread. Plain, ordinary bread."

I'm sure that whatever perplexity they may have felt was soon lost in the continuing of the meal, because now they went on eating. And I'm sure the conversation progressed too, in its own peculiar way—the way conversations usually unfold, without particular order, design, or logic. When the meal was complete, Jesus took the cup of wine and said, "This cup that is poured out for you is the new covenant in my blood" (Luke 22:20). The better part of a meal, and a miasma of conversation, had elapsed since they had eaten the bread. The only thing that tied the two little incidents together is the way Jesus referred to the two elements as his body and his blood.

This second statement, about the wine, must have seemed to the disciples as enigmatic as the earlier statement about the bread. And all the more so because Jesus spoke of the wine as "the new covenant in my blood." The disciples were good Jews; they knew about God's covenant, and of course they knew that truly serious covenants were sealed with blood. But it was always the blood of animals. Whatever did Jesus mean by a *new* covenant? And whatever in the world did he mean by the covenant being not in the blood of a bull, a goat, or a lamb, but in Jesus' own blood? Still more, the disciples were being told to drink it. It must have seemed very strange, especially to Jews, whose holy law forbade eating or drinking blood.

But before they could ponder further, Jesus announced that he was going to be betrayed, and that the betrayer was with them at the table. The conversation continued a while longer. Jesus taught them about several things and warned Peter that he would deny his Lord. Then the group adjourned to the Mount of Olives, and from that moment on it was a kaleidoscopic series of events, one tumbling wildly upon another: prayer in Gethsemane, arrest, trials, and crucifixion.

If you had been there that night, do you think you would have remembered the communion event, out of that bewildering complex of happenings? Would you have seen a memorable connection between the moment when Jesus broke bread, early in the evening, and referred to it as his broken body, and then later his passing the cup and speaking of it as his blood—when between the two events there was so much talk? And would you have been confounded that Jesus suggested eating his body and drinking his blood? And would you have thought it strange that Judas ate the bread and drank the cup—the Body, the Blood—then went out and betrayed Jesus?

Perhaps it is no wonder that we so often come to this table—the Communion table—and leave it, without sensing the magnitude of what has happened. Malcolm Muggeridge, the British journalist and television personality who came to Christian faith after years as an agnostic, recalls some of his feelings when, as a young student at Cambridge, he hoped to find something uniquely moving in the sacrament. At the time, he longed to "walk back to his seat in the congregation in a kind of trance. But this does not happen; he is as wide awake on his return journey from the altar rail as on making his way to it" (*Confessions of a Twentieth-Century Pilgrim*, 33-34). And many a modern communicant would confess the same longing, and perhaps the same disappointment. After all, the ceremony is really so very simple.

And yet, it is so extraordinary that there is probably no hour of the day or night when there is not someone, somewhere, kneeling at this Table. Year after year, century after century, it is so. If you and I had been at the table that evening nearly twenty centuries ago, could we have imagined, even remotely, how significant that table would someday become? That people would someday refer to it, in every part of the world, simply as "the Table of our Lord"?

There is, after all, no table like it. This table reaches from that upper room in Jerusalem all the way through cathedrals in Europe and America, to the place where you will next take the sacrament. This table is revered in mud hut churches in Africa, where people speak the sacred words in languages you and I have never heard. It has often been set up, in crude fashion, in the darkest pits of confinement, where people imprisoned for their faith in Christ have saved a fragment of bread and a spoonful of water just so they can say, "His body. His blood." And they do it with a triumph that shakes the dungeon walls.

The first time I sat at this table, it was in a tiny Methodist church in downtown Sioux City, Iowa—the Helping Hand Mission. But since then I have sat at this table in great auditoriums in Nairobi, Kenya, and in Singapore, surrounded by nearly one hundred flags, representing the countries where some form of the Methodist, or Wesleyan, movement exists. And as I sat in those gatherings, I reminded myself that the Methodist movement is only one small segment of the huge body of persons all over the world called Christians, and that virtually all of those bodies choose to honor this table.

So I ponder that once, long ago, there was a table, where thirteen men sat. The number itself haunts us, because since there were thirteen at that table, and one of them betrayed his Lord, people have ever since thought of the number thirteen as being unlucky.

But who could have imagined that night that where thirteen sat at the table, hundreds of millions would sit at the same table, two millennia later, everywhere on this planet. And someone will say, "The body of our Lord. The blood of Christ, shed for you." And in that moment, eternity will break in upon human souls. At a common piece of furniture called a table, you and I will eat a crumb of bread, we will drink from a cup, and for that moment, all of the company of heaven will observe in splendid awe. Such a table! Such a table!

CHAPTER 9

The Full Tomb

JOHN 20:1-18: Early on the first day of the week, while it was still dark, Mary Magdalene came to the tomb and saw that the stone had been removed from the tomb. So she ran and went to Simon Peter and the other disciple, the one whom Jesus loved, and said to them, "They have taken the Lord out of the tomb, and we do not know where they have laid him." Then Peter and the other disciple set out and went toward the tomb. The two were running together, but the other disciple outran Peter and reached the tomb first. He bent down to look in and saw the linen wrappings lying there, but he did not go in. Then Simon Peter came, following him, and went into the tomb. He saw the linen wrappings lying there, and the cloth that had been on Jesus' head, not lying with the linen wrappings but rolled up in a place by itself. Then the other disciple, who reached the tomb first, also went in, and he saw and believed;

for as yet they did not understand the scripture, that he must rise from the dead. Then the disciples returned to their homes.

But Mary stood weeping outside the tomb. As she wept, she bent over to look into the tomb; and she saw two angels in white, sitting where the body of Jesus had been lying, one at the head and the other at the feet. They said to her, "Woman, why are you weeping?" She said to them, "They have taken away my Lord, and I do not know where they have laid him." When she had said this, she turned around and saw Jesus standing there, but she did not know that it was Jesus. Jesus said to her, "Woman, why are you weeping? Whom are you looking for?" Supposing him to be the gardener, she said to him, "Sir, if you have carried him away, tell me where you have laid him, and I will take him away. Jesus said to her, "Mary!" She turned and said to him in Hebrew, "Rabbouni!"

(which means Teacher). Jesus said to her, "Do not hold on to me, because I have not yet ascended to the Father. But go to my brothers and say to them, 'I am ascending to my Father and your Father, to my God and your God.'" Mary Magdalene went and announced to the disciples, "I have seen the Lord"; and she told them that he had said these things to her.

I wonder how many books and pamphlets have been written about the empty tomb? Or even more, how many sermons have been preached on this theme? The empty tomb is a favorite subject for poets and artists. If I should ask you to describe from your imagination a picture that symbolizes Easter, almost surely one of the scenes that would come to your mind would be a stone tomb with a huge rock rolled back from its entrance, with the implied message that the tomb is empty. *The empty tomb.* The phrase itself captures us. It seems symbolic of all that Easter means.

And yet, it isn't to the point.

It surely wasn't the point on the first Easter morning. The first person to come to Jesus' tomb on that most memorable of mornings was Mary Magdalene. When she arrived, "while it was still dark," she saw that the stone had been removed from the entrance to the tomb. The sight did not fill her with excitement and hope, as we now infer when we use the phrase, "the empty tomb." Quite the contrary. For Mary, it was a scene of desolation. As she reported it to Simon Peter and "the other disciple" (probably John), "They have taken the Lord out of the tomb, and we do not know where they have laid him" (John 20:2). It must have seemed that the enemies of Jesus had inflicted still another indignity upon him. It was not enough, apparently, that they had scourged him publicly and had crucified him; now they were even treating his corpse with disdain, moving it as soon as possible to some other place. Now Mary could not even fulfill her humble act of continuing devotion, since there was not a body to receive her gift of love.

Nor did the enemies of Jesus see any problem in explaining an empty tomb. It was quite simple: Just say that the disciples of Jesus had come at some time when the guards were asleep and had stolen the body away (see Matthew 28:11-15). Of itself, an empty tomb would soon be forgotten.

So neither the enemies of Jesus nor the friends of Jesus (with the possible exception of the impetuous Peter) were—respectively—afraid of, or impressed by, an empty tomb. Ultimately an empty tomb proves nothing, except that it is empty. The empty tomb makes a movingly poignant picture for those who believe, and it is a convenient shorthand phrase to symbolize the Resurrection. But if the essence of the Easter story were nothing more than an empty tomb, the whole matter would have been forgotten years ago.

Perhaps that's because tombs are always empty. Yes, they have bodies in them, but the bodies are in such a condition that we describe them with a special term—corpse. In many of our modern graves, we have quite beautiful caskets and secure burial vaults. Nevertheless, the tombs are empty. They have no hope, no true laughter, no singing. Not, at least, until Jesus came, and broke the power of death. And he did that by *filling* the tomb.

Because if a tomb is anything, it is the ultimate expression of emptiness. This is something of the poignancy of much of the book of Ecclesiastes. The writer is describing a life without Easter, and his definitive word for it is *vanity*—"emptiness." "What do people gain," he asks, "from all the toil / at which they toil under the sun?" (Ecclesiastes 1:3). "All things are wearisome" (Ecclesiastes 1:8), because they all end in a tomb. So the writer methodically and mercilessly goes through the things for which people live, from sex and success to culture and learning, and concludes that they all end in emptiness. It's all a matter of people living "the few days of their vain life," days that "pass like a shadow" (Ecclesiastes 6:12). So the writer sees life as an emptiness because—since he had no perception of the Easter-yet-to-come—it was going to end in an empty tomb.

So here's the good news about Easter. The tomb was now full. And it has been full ever since.

Victory, for instance. One of Charles Wesley's great hymns challenges the domain of the tomb by a series of questions: "Where, O death, is now thy sting? . . . Where's thy victory, boasting grave?" ("Christ the Lord Is Risen Today"). Tombs have for so long declared themselves the ultimate winners; after all, no mortal escapes them! But no longer. We do indeed die, but with a sublime confidence that we will rise again. We will win! Our Lord has taken conquest of the grave, turning its emptiness into a habitation of victory. The game we humans have been losing since Adam and Eve is now turned into victory.

And hope too. The tomb is now full of hope. During my nearly forty years as a parish pastor, I stood many hundreds of times at the open grave, speaking the words of committal, and knowing that as soon as our gathering left the cemetery, workers would lower the vault into the ground and would begin to throw dirt upon it. But I conducted such "final rites" with hope. As a fellow human being, I wanted often to weep with the mourners, and sometimes I did; I felt for their loss, particularly in those instances where death seemed to have come earlier than was its right. But my tears were of sympathy, not of despair. The tomb is now full of hope. I remember my father pausing for the last time at the casket of my mother and saying quietly, "I'll see you in the morning, Mother," and I knew he was right. Such is our hope. Simple, yes; but full and sure.

Allow me for a moment to turn the camera of eternity another way, while I observe that the tomb is also, since Easter, full of despair. Not human despair, but hell's despair. Call the ultimate enemies of humankind what you will; I shall encompass them all in the word *hell*, while I promise you that hell lost at the tomb. And ever since, as hell approaches our tombs—hell, in its many guises of fear, hate, dread, and despair—hell *itself* is filled with despair. The game is not yet over, but the final score has been announced. Hell has lost.

So it's a full tomb. Full of life, hope, prospect, glory, gladness, anticipation.

How full?

So full that the small body of first-century believers, who seemed ripe for immediate extinction, became instead a movement of such proportions that within less than a generation their enemies were referring to them as the people who were turning the world upside down (Acts 17:6). The odds were so dramatically against the little company of believers. Nearly all of the learning and leadership of the Jewish people had united against Jesus, and the Roman government had quite readily implemented the desires of this influential group. Although some few wealthy women had become believers, and at least two notable men, Nicodemus and Joseph of Arimathea, the leadership of the believers was an unimpressive lot. They were modestly educated, at best, with no experience at organizing a movement or dealing with the wider world. When Jesus told his group of fishermen, small-business people, and day laborers that they should go into all the world to preach the gospel, I doubt that there was anyone in the group who knew anything about the world beyond a fifty-mile radius. They were an absurd minority, with nothing going for them. Except that they were *full*.

And, of course, they had every reason to go into hiding. With their leader, Jesus, crucified in the fashion of a criminal, they couldn't help wondering when they might suffer the same fate. They had kept a somewhat safe distance at the crucifixion, but they must still have overheard the mocking of the crowds. I'm astonished that they were willing to make themselves open to the same kind of rejection, and perhaps even the same kind of death.

But the fullness that had come to these believers was of such abundance and quality that they met humiliating martyrdoms and emerged with nothing less than divine poise. Look at the first of this company of martyrs, Stephen. A man of limited background, he dared to challenge the best religious minds of his time, and so shocked them with his passion and insight that they could find no way to cope with him except to kill him. And even as they did so, he prayed, "Lord, do not hold this sin against them" (Acts 7:60). A grand fullness brought Stephen to his victorious dying; moments before the had "gazed into heaven," and declared, "I see the heavens opened and the Son of Man standing at the right hand of God!" (Acts 7:55-56). Confronting such a person, the enemies must have sensed their own pathetic emptiness. How could they compete with someone so full?

Stephen began an army of martyrs that extends even to our own day. No wonder it is said that "the blood of the martyrs is the seed of the church." If those who have tried to destroy Christianity by killing its followers have any measure of reason, they must feel quite disheartened. Persecution has never wiped out the church; how can it, when its people have found the wonder of the full tomb? These courageous souls, of whom most of us feel completely unworthy, have made their persecutors look ridiculous.

There's a certain logic in all of this. With death banished, there is room in the tomb for all that is good and hopeful. Take from the tomb the despair and hopelessness, the loneliness and frustration, the sense of meaninglessness and of dread, and suddenly there is room and to spare for life in its fullness.

What a wonderful reversal this is—or perhaps I should say, a setting right. In the normal pattern, death and its minions are always crowding out our plans and dreams. In my years as a pastor I so often had conversations with the bereaved where someone said, "We had always planned to buy a little property in the South for our retirement, but this has changed all of that." Or, "We were looking forward so much to visiting our children and grandchildren more often, but those dreams are no more." Indeed! Death crowds out some of the loveliest of our expectations; and if there had not been an Easter, all of our human stories would have to stop at such a dismal place, with goodness and dreams crowded out by the emptiness of death. But Easter has righted this matter. With the emptiness of death gone, there is room now for hope beyond the grave, and words beyond the farewell at the funeral or memorial service.

In an amusing, ironical way, the shrines of the Holy Land show how full the tomb now is. The traveler who wants to see the sacred places in Israel and the Middle East can see the place where tradition says that Jesus was born, and any number of sites recalling events in his life and ministry. But when you want to visit the place of the Resurrection, you find two sites on your pilgrimage map. The first, in the Church of the Holy Sepulchre, is probably best authenticated by archaeologists, but the Garden Tomb near Gordon's Calvary often appeals more to the average visitor. In any event, I am never troubled by the fact that there are two possible sites. I realize, of course, that ancient sites are very difficult to prove beyond error. But more than that, the believer in me smiles with the thought that the Easter event is in fact too big to hold to one location.

Nearly twenty centuries of generations have now slipped by since our Lord was raised from the dead, and millions upon millions of believers have visited the tomb—some in person, and most by faith and sacred imagination. And at that tomb, they have been filled. For the power of this place and what it represents is so great that it will fill the emptiness of the human race for as long as life shall last.

Remember always that emptiness is the antithesis of Jesus Christ and of the faith that he represents and inspires. He said that he came that we might have life, and "have it abundantly" (John 10:10). For all of the emptiness of life, for all of its vanity and disappointment, Jesus Christ is not only the answer, he is the antithesis. This is why, when I look at his Jerusalem tomb, I think it full. Fullness is our Savior's name.

CHAPTER 10

At the Corner of Today and Forever

ACTS 16:16-34: One day, as we were going to the place of prayer, we met a slave-girl who had a spirit of divination and brought her owners a great deal of money by fortune-telling. While she followed Paul and us, she would cry out, "These men are slaves of the Most High God, who proclaim to you a way of salvation." She kept doing this for many days. But Paul, very much annoyed, turned and said to the spirit, "I order you in the name of Jesus Christ to come out of her." And it came out that very hour.

But when her owners saw that their hope of making money was gone, they seized Paul and Silas and dragged them into the marketplace before the authorities. When they had brought them before the magistrates, they said, "These men are disturbing our city; they are Jews and are advocating customs that are not lawful for us as Romans to adopt or observe." The crowd joined in attacking them, and the magistrates had them stripped of their clothing and ordered them to be beaten with rods. After they had given them a severe flogging, they threw them into prison and ordered the jailer to keep them securely. Following these instructions, he put them in the innermost cell and fastened their feet in the stocks.

About midnight Paul and Silas were praying and singing hymns to God, and the prisoners were listening to them. Suddenly there was an earthquake, so violent that the foundations of the prison were shaken; and immediately all the doors were opened and everyone's chains were unfastened. When the jailer woke up and saw the prison doors wide open, he drew his sword and was about to kill himself, since he supposed that the prisoners had escaped. But Paul shouted in a loud voice, "Do not harm yourself, for we are all here." The jailer called for lights, and rushing in, he fell down trembling before Paul and Silas. Then he brought them outside and said, "Sirs, what must I do to be saved?" they answered, "Believe on the Lord Jesus, and you will be saved, you and your household." They spoke the word of the Lord to him and to all who were in his house. At the same hour of the night he took them and washed their wounds; then he and his entire family were baptized without delay. He brought them up into the house and set food before them; and he and his entire household rejoiced that he had become a believer in God.

I love life, and I have no strong complaint about the way life has treated me. Yes, I've had a share of pain, but I've brought most of it on myself, and the pain I've had doesn't compare with what I've seen some other persons suffer.

Nevertheless, if God should ever ask my opinion as to how this world should be run, I would make one suggestion. I would recommend that at certain points in the journey of life there be erected signs stating clearly, *Warning: Dangerous Intersection*. Perhaps I wouldn't heed the warning, and maybe you wouldn't either. But I wish at least that we might be warned.

I am uneasy with the fact that at any moment of any day I may encounter some issue of eternity without knowing that it is coming. I wish someone would warn us that just up ahead—an hour from now, or at seven this evening—*Today* will intersect *Forever*. I repeat, if I had such knowledge, I'm not sure what I would do about it, but I wish I might have some warning.

The best poets and novelists have always been intrigued by this intersection. Gerard Manley Hopkins saw it as a reason for worshipful wonder: "The world," he said, "is charged with the grandeur of God." On every hand, at every juncture in our path, lie wonder and majesty. Charles Williams, that remarkable twentieth-century British writer, wrote novels that are called "supernatural thrillers," because Williams was possessed by the feeling that the line between us and another world is so thin that we never know when or to what degree that other world may be intersecting with ours. Someone has said that Williams saw demons or angels behind every bush.

This sense of the eternal potential in every moment is so real that we celebrate it in ways that are both sentimental and absurd. The lyricist has given the idea a romantic turn, telling us that on "some enchanted evening" we may see someone "across a crowded room," and that we'll know "even then" that somehow we'll see them "again and again." This is part and parcel, I'm sure, of the mind-set that makes some people—several million of them, in fact—read the astrology column in their newspaper each day; they have the insistent feeling that this day just may, possibly, be an unforgettable one. Some people celebrate the mood I'm describing by the words they stick on their refrigerator door: "This is the first day of the rest of your life."

Well, this is, indeed, the way it is. This interval of time in which we're now living, called *Today*, may intersect at some crucial point on that highway called *Forever*. Nor should we be surprised that we sense that this is so. It is our instinctive testimony to a conviction that we are eternal creatures. Something in us (something that I dare to feel has been planted in us by God) senses that we *matter*, and that we matter profoundly. Except for moments of irrational despair, we can't believe that we are just meaningless creatures, living out short and meaningless days on a meaningless planet. Something very deep within us insists that we matter; indeed, specifically, that we matter to *God*. So we feel that perhaps today, or any day, we may have an encounter that will affect all of the rest of our lives—and, perhaps, even eternity. We sense that we not only have the capacity to encounter the corner of Today and Forever, but that such encounters are inevitable. So shouldn't there be a warning for such an intersection as that?

It is this realization, this conviction, that draws me to a man who lived some nineteen centuries ago. I can't tell you his name, yet I feel I know him well. He was a civil servant in the Roman government. To be specific, he was the jailer in the city of Philippi. You may think that was a job of no great moment, but in at least one way, it was a vitally important job. Important, that is, in that it was a life-and-death job. It is generally understood that in those days a jailer paid with his own person for any prisoners who escaped, suffering their penalty upon himself. I can't help wondering why anyone would want such a job. Perhaps it is a measure of this man that he was either so desperate for work that would support his family or so challenged by the daily ultimates of what he did that he would assume such a post as this. Perhaps it is the same combination of despair and daring that motivates generations of coal miners, who insert themselves time and again into shafts that measure only in inches, even though they know neighbors and relatives who have died in the same pursuit.

Most of the time, the jailer's work was pretty grim. The jail itself was not a pretty place, and the people who inhabited it were usually the flotsam and jetsam of life. Now the truth is, most of us tend slowly to become like our environment; indeed, it is astonishing if we do not. I think therefore that we can rightly assume that this man must have become a hard man. Not necessarily brutal or unfair, but tough to the core. Working day by day in an environment of despair, threat, and dark loneliness must surely have taken its toll on the very essence of this man. Still worse, he and his family had to live right there in the prison complex. He could never fully get away from his domain of ugliness.

And yet, something about the job must have held the man. After all, it was a position of responsibility, and responsibility ties a strong cord to a person's soul. So it was that he made his way on a particular morning from his dwelling to his work. He looked in on each prisoner—a typically sorry lot—and began to deal with the minutiae of the day. It was like every day, a day called *Today.*

But sometime that afternoon the authorities appeared with two bloody, naked figures. They were so badly beaten that he hardly noticed anything distinctive about their appearance, even if any such distinctiveness existed. The men were delivered with a message of some urgency: The officials warned the jailer that he should not by any means allow these two men to escape. I venture the jailer smiled; these two men didn't look like the escaping type. With no more thought, he put them into the most secure spot in his prison, the inner dungeon; and just to make matters still more sure, he clamped their feet in the stocks.

That night, around midnight, the two men began singing. I doubt that their song made much of an impression on the jailer, except that it was causing the other prisoners to be silent. And, yes, the jailer must surely have noticed that the song was religious, though he may not have recognized many of its specifics; and the song seemed to indicate that the men were happy. As a matter of fact, they sounded as if they had just returned victorious from the Olympics.

And then, the jailer's whole world caved in. An earthquake struck. By the time the tremors had subsided, the jailer realized that all of is prisoners had been shaken loose from their stocks. This was the worst that could happen to him. His career and his very life were finished. He drew his sword to kill himself, feeling he'd rather do the job himself than to be put through the shame of a trial before the government executed him.

But just as quickly, his despair was interrupted by a call from one of those strange, singing prisoners: "Don't do it! We are all here!" The jailer ran to the dungeon and fell down before the two men. Then he led them out of their pit so he could ask them a poignant question: *Sirs, what must I do to be saved?*

What did the jailer mean by his question? Someone who is accustomed to meeting life at a completely secular level answers, "It's very simple. He's wondering how to get out of the mess he's in. You know—his job, the peril of losing the other prisoners, and perhaps even his execution." Now, without being unduly unkind or overly pious, I have to challenge this analysis. Frankly, I don't think my secular friend has looked deeply enough into this story, or into human nature as a whole.

So now we seek an answer from a religious person. He is equally sure that it's a simple matter. "Very simple; this man is hungry for eternal life. He wants to be saved, just like he says. It's clear as can be." And again, without being abrupt, or without seeming disrespectful of his religion, I have to tell my devout friend that he has read too much into the story.

You see, I think we're dealing with an instance where someone is standing at the corner of Today and Forever. Here's what I mean. On the one hand, we religious folks are inclined to see everything happening on that Forever Street; everything is eternal, with folks waiting to be saved and sanctified. But to be honest about it, most people aren't walking around every day wondering how to be saved. If they were, we preachers would have an easier time of it. Most people, most of the time, are thinking about *Today:* about keeping their job, getting a ticket for some playoff game, wondering about their sex life, or calculating whether their mutual funds are going to pay off properly.

But on the other hand, secular people think that that's *all* there is to life. They feel that if a person can just keep up mortgage payments, have a few friends, get an occasional promotion, and see their kids make a Little League team, they've got it all.

Then, one day something happens that brings life to the intersection of Today and Forever. For that jailer, nineteen centuries ago, it was two unlikely prisoners, followed by an earthquake. Sometimes it's bad news from the doctor, or a violation by your spouse or your best friend, or flunking out of college.

At such times, we're likely to cry out, "What must I do to be saved?" But of course we don't usually say it that way. We say, "What am I going to do next? Whatever in the world am

I going to do?" Or, contrariwise, the intersection may come when everything is really going quite well, but you find yourself saying, "There must be more to life than this. More than three cars and a promotion and a retirement plan. There must be more." That's a cry just as authentic and just as poignant as when the jailer at Philippi said, "What must I do to be saved?" The verbs aren't really any different.

It is at such moments that Today and Forever intersect. We think at first that the issue is our job, that broken relationship, or that lump that may be malignant. But for a human being, nothing on this earth is *simply* on this earth. Everything that happens to us has some possible significance for eternity.

That's because you and I are eternal creatures. So when the jailer says to his two prisoners, Paul and Silas, "What must I do to be saved?" he may at first be thinking simply and solely about keeping his job—"How do I get out of the mess I'm in?" But the crisis in his work opens the door to the recognition that he is more than just a jailer, more than just a job-keeper, more even than just a husband and father. He is an eternal creature—one who happens to spend his time on this planet running a jail, providing for his family, and paying his taxes. But don't let these details confuse you. Primarily and above all, this man is an eternal creature. Just like you. And me.

So Paul and Silas said, "Believe on the Lord Jesus, and you will be saved, along with your entire household" (Acts 16:31). Now that was an eternal answer, but it wasn't just a heavenly answer. Because eternity doesn't mean simply pie in the sky when you die, it also means a different quality of life right here and now. Recognizing that the intersecting street is *Forever* doesn't diminish the importance of *Today*. To the contrary, Today now carries more meaning than ever, because its eternal element has been acknowledged.

Consider, for instance, that although the jailer asked only about his own salvation, Paul and Silas's answer included his "entire household." When we touch eternity, we get a more profound understanding of our responsibility to family, neighbor, and society.

Indeed, see what happened next to that jailer. After listening to what Paul and Silas had to say, he noticed something that he hadn't seen the day before when the two men were brought to the jail. He realized that they were covered with blood and lacerations, and that these wounds ought to be washed and bound up. So he did just that. That's because Forever had touched his Today, and he was now a different kind of man, with a different sense of responsibility for Today. So the jailer performed a baptism of kindness on Paul and Silas, and they reciprocated with a baptism of sacrament for him and his family.

Later that day, Paul and Silas left town. The jailer went back to running his jail. But the Bible says that he and his whole family now "rejoiced because they all believed in God" (Acts 16:34 NLT). And from that day on, I venture that everything was indeed different. He was still a jailer, still a husband and father, still a citizen. But one who, through Jesus Christ, had established his relationship with God and eternity.

So as I was saying earlier, probably Life ought to put up a warning sign at certain points: *Dangerous Intersection*. Because you never know when such a juncture might be coming up. You arise one morning, thinking it will be just another day, never guessing what may be ahead. Business with God. Eternal business.

Believe me, it could happen to you. Perhaps it already has. Or perhaps it will sometime later this month, or this week. Maybe even today. Quite possibly today.

CHAPTER *11*

Going Easter Shopping

COLOSSIANS 3:5-14: Put to death, therefore, whatever in you is earthly: fornication, impurity, passion, evil desire, and greed (which is idolatry). On account of these the wrath of God is coming on those who are disobedient. These are the ways you also once followed, when you were living that life. But now you must get rid of all such things—anger, wrath, malice, slander, and abusive language from your mouth. Do not lie to one another, seeing that you have stripped off the old self with its practices and have clothed yourselves with the new self, which is being renewed in knowledge according to the image of its creator. In that renewal there is no longer Greek and Jew, circumcised and uncircumcised, barbarian, Scythian, slave and free; but Christ is all and in all!

As God's chosen ones, holy and beloved, clothe yourselves with compassion, kindness, humility, meekness, and patience. Bear with one another and, if anyone has a complaint against another, forgive each other; just as the Lord has forgiven you, so you also must forgive. Above all, clothe yourselves with love, which binds everything together in perfect harmony.

If I may, I'd like to take you Easter shopping. I confess that this is an unlikely invitation, since I'm not one of the world's greatest shoppers. Actually, I avoid malls as much as possible. Besides, I belong to a profession, the clergy, that has been known in some generations for being unsympathetic with Easter shopping. In the 1920s, when all women wore hats to church, and when those hats reached their glorious best on Easter Sunday, a popular preacher in New York City, John Roach Stratton, looked out upon his congregation and observed that he wasn't sure whether he was looking down on a fruit orchard or a poultry yard.

And yet, in truth, nowhere was the Easter parade celebrated more variously than on the steps of ten thousand churches across America. Irving Berlin may have memorialized the parade for New York's Fifth Avenue, but that was only the tip of the celebratory iceberg. The greatest parade has always taken place in churches large and small, urban, small town, and rural, where several hundred thousand little girls appear in their finest, while others say with unfeigned delight, "Now don't you look nice!"

My intention is neither to defend nor to celebrate such a practice, which is probably just as well, since I'm sure no one cares about my opinions in this matter. But it is appropriate to observe that Easter outfits have a long and significant history. One tradition says that in the early days of the Christian church, baptism was celebrated at Easter, and that all of the persons who were to be baptized wore spotless white robes as a sign of their new life in Christ. And every year thereafter, they would wear their best new clothes to commemorate the wonder of that Sunday when they were baptized into their faith in Christ.

It's easy to believe this tradition, because the Bible so often uses clothing as a figure of speech to describe the Christian life. In one instance, the apostle Paul speaks of dressing ourselves in "the whole armor of God" (Ephesians 6:10-17). He uses the same kind of language in his letter to the Colossians, when he compares the Christian experience to a change of clothing. "You have stripped off the old self with its practices," Paul writes, "and have clothed yourselves with the new self" (Colossians 3:9-10). And he lists those things that we should be done with: anger, wrath, malice, slander, abusive language, and lying (Colossians 3:8-9).

Then the apostle describes the new wardrobe: "As God's

chosen ones, holy and beloved, *clothe* yourselves [emphasis added] with compassion, kindness, humility, meekness, and patience" (Colossians 3:12). So Paul is recommending a change in wardrobe; take off the old outfit, he urges, and put on this new one. I'm reminded of a spiritual that I heard long ago: "I'm going to tell you the best thing that I ever do: / I took off the old robe, and put on the new."

But such a process of change doesn't come about easily. Most of us become rather comfortable in the spiritual garments we wear; so much so that we hardly recognize that there's anything inappropriate or unattractive about them. And as for the new outfit that the apostle recommends— well, where can you find it? The answer, I think, is clear. Only in the Resurrection Shop. Garments like goodness, patience, and compassion aren't to be found just anywhere. I dare to suggest that they wouldn't be on the moral market in any impressive way if it weren't for the change that came to our planet with Christ's victory at Calvary.

So follow me, if you will, into the Resurrection Shop. The experience isn't entirely unlike what I've known from time to time in my search for a new suit at a department store or a men's clothing store. On such shopping excursions, I dress my best—perhaps in the same mood that causes some folks to clean their house before the cleaning service arrives! But I always receive a shock when I'm only a few feet from the clerk. My necktie goes awry, a shirt collar pops up, my trousers lose their crease and my shoes their shine.

For years, I didn't understand this phenomenon. Now I know that it happens because of the prospect of the three-way mirror. I look reasonably acceptable if I choose my approach to a straight mirror, but a three-way mirror allows no such posturing. It reveals facts about my anatomy that I otherwise have chosen to forget. I have the same experience in the Resurrection Shop. Out on the "street," I don't look too bad. True, I'm sometimes impatient, but not compared to the people I like to compare myself to. And I know that my thoughts aren't always the best, but I like to entertain the impression that they are still above the average.

But in the Resurrection Shop, I find myself facing a different standard. The mirror of God's Word reveals insights into my person that I can ignore when I compare myself with others. Because in the Resurrection Shop I am compared not with other people, but with Jesus Christ. Standing beside him, I realize how poorly outfitted I am, and how badly I need to do some high-powered shopping. So I approach the Holy Spirit, who directs the shop.

—I know I need something new, but I hope you'll understand the limits of my price range.

"Everything in this shop is within your ability to buy, if you're only willing to pay the price."

—Please tell me what you have.

"Let me show you a garment called compassion."

—Is that something new, fresh on the market this season?

"Not really. But when Paul first recommended it some twenty seasons ago, it was almost unheard of. Much of his first-century world seemed oblivious to human suffering; the maimed and the sick, the aged, the physically weak and those unable to care for themselves were easily shunted aside. But Jesus looked out on the nondescript crowds, so many of whom were limited in some fashion or other, and responded with compassion. A new force had been set loose in the world."

—I wonder if it would matter in our time?

"Compassion fatigue. Your world talks about compassion fatigue. Your culture sees so much need by way of television—starving children in Africa, bodies piled like cord wood in places where so-called ethnic cleansing is going on—and their capacity for compassion seems to be exhausted."

—I've noticed the feeling with city panhandlers.

"Exactly. You learn, as a defensive city dweller, that you can't help every beggar, so you avoid their eyes. A person's natural capacity for compassion will soon run out unless one gets a resurrection garment."

—What you say is interesting, but I'd like to see some of the rest of your stock.

"By all means. Here's an item we call *kindness*. Somehow it's never out of date. To do it justice, I should show you the Greek label: *chrestotes*. This means the virtue of a person whose neighbor's good is as dear to him or her as their own. Have you noticed that goodness sometimes has rather hard, severe lines? *Chrestotes* saves us from that danger, because kindness has gentle lines. Someone once said of the great Quaker Rufus Jones, that to meet him in the morning was to feel set up for the day. That's a mark of the person who's wearing kindness. And of course this kind of person runs entirely contrary to society's contemporary patterns. Ever heard of 'snob appeal'? This is the opposite of Christian kindness. Snob appeal depends on our having something the other person can't get. *Chrestotes* says, 'I like this so much that I want you to have it too.'"

—I'll admit that's not natural.

"Not natural at all. That's why the apostle Paul pictured it as the kind of virtue that comes from a life of faith. You can't get it just anywhere."

—Did Paul recommend anything else?

"Yes. In the same fashion statement that he outlined for the church at Colossae, he recommended *humility*."

—That wouldn't really work for me. You see, I'm struggling to build up my ego. I don't need anything to bring me down.

"That's a common misconception in your world. Your culture says, 'If you've got it, flaunt it.' Such an attitude shows insecurity. Those who are at peace with themselves don't find it necessary to put on a show."

—So what is humility?

"Humility isn't a cringing, servile thing. Remember Uriah Heep from *David Copperfield*? Well, that's not humility. In truth, a person with humility knows what he or she has, but knows where he got it—and knows also that others have some gifts that he doesn't have. Take your friend Albin.

He's a magnificent organist and pianist. If he were to say that he can't play the piano, it wouldn't be humility, it would be a denial of God's generous gift. Albin shows humility when he interrupts a concert to introduce the piano and organ teacher of his youth. He knows he has talent, but he knows where he got it, and he knows who helped him to develop it still further."

—I guess I wouldn't look so bad in humility. I'm afraid I never really considered its possibilities.

"You, and a good many others. But before you leave our shop, let me show you something else that Paul recommended. It's another article with a Greek label. You call it *gentleness*, but the Greeks called it *praotes*. (See Colossians 3:12, NIV; translated as *meekness* in NRSV.) Aristotle said that *praotes* was the perfect mean between too little anger and too much anger."

—But I thought anger was always bad.

"Not at all. No reform movement would ever have happened if someone hadn't gotten angry about the state of things as they found them. It was when people grew angry about slavery that its death knell was sounded. So, too, with child labor.

"But the problem is to harness that anger. That's where *praotes*—*gentleness*—comes in. Anger destroys even in the name of great causes; without restraint, anger will defeat the very matters it endorses. And our usual brand of self-control won't make it. As William Barclay used to say, we need to be God-controlled. That's gentleness. Because gentleness is power under purposeful direction."

—I just noticed those beautiful garments that are being offered at a reduced price! What are they?

"*Patience.* There's no lovelier item anywhere."

—Just what I'd like to get for several of the people nearest to me!

"Sorry! Nothing in this shop can be bought for others. Every article here is custom made, and the purchaser must get it for himself or herself. But it's interesting about patience. Most people feel that if those around them were more patient, many problems would be solved. Somehow they rarely recognize that patience might be appropriate for their own Christian wardrobe.

"Circumstances ought to prove otherwise. A few difficult coworkers, a spouse that seems to have developed an unpleasant mannerism, an occasional morning traffic jam, and one would think that patience would be pursued vigorously. After all, consider what a lovely world it would be if everyone were more patient. But of course, patience isn't a natural virtue. Because to be patient, one must be thinking of the other person; and sometimes patience requires one to realize that the other person might even be in the right.

"And one more thing. Our fashion expert, Paul, said that we should round out our wardrobe with *love*. 'And over all these virtues put on love, which binds them all together in perfect unity' (Colossians 3:14). Love completes the resurrection wardrobe; it brings together all of the other wonderful elements so that each one takes on still more beauty and significance."

—Paul was quite a fashion expert, wasn't he!

"Well, not always. When we first met him, when he was familiarly known as Saul of Tarsus, he was wearing one of the most outlandish outfits you can imagine. It was a mishmash of ethnic pride, intellectual arrogance, and spiritual self-righteousness. But once he got into the Resurrection Shop, he's been coming back ever since."

—Wait a minute. Are you saying that one trip isn't enough?

"Let me ask you a question in return. How old were you when you gave your life to Christ?"

—Not quite eleven. Just a boy.

"What were you wearing that night?"

—Some knickers. I remember that especially. And a shirt my mother had made for me. And the only shoes I had.

"Are you still wearing the same clothes now?"

—Forgive me for laughing, but I'd look pretty ridiculous wearing those clothes today.

"Then what makes you think your original spiritual garments should still be adequate? A person's spiritual wardrobe needs constant updating. The humility or patience that looked good a few days ago can easily be a little worn-looking after a difficult week. That's why we need to get to church regularly, to do a little holy shopping. As a matter of fact, once a week is hardly enough!"

Wouldn't it be wonderful if we commented more often on the spiritual wardrobes our friends are wearing? Somehow we find it easier to say, "I love your new dress," or "Where did you get that necktie?" than to say, "Your gentleness is beautiful." And I suppose we're also a little fearful that if we comment about someone's patience or humility, it might seem to suggest that the person wasn't doing that well previously.

Still, wouldn't it be nice if people commented more often about the Easter wardrobe? The *real* Easter wardrobe, that is. Wouldn't it be nice if someone were to say to you, "Is that your new Easter outfit?" And you could reply, "Yes, it's some of the latest *kindness*. Paul spoke of it in his letter to the Colossians. See the cut, the fit...?"

And your friend answers, "It looks as if it were made just for you."

To which you can answer, "It was! At Calvary, and in the Garden. It's Easter clothing, and you buy it in the Resurrection Shop."

I'm going to tell you the best thing that I ever do:
I took off the old robe, and put on the new.

CHAPTER *12*

The Lion and the Lamb

REVELATION 5:1-14: Then I saw in the right hand of the one seated on the throne a scroll written on the inside and on the back, sealed with seven seals; and I saw a mighty angel proclaiming with a loud voice, "Who is worthy to open the scroll and break its seals?" And no one in heaven or on earth or under the earth was able to open the scroll or to look into it. And I began to weep bitterly because no one was found worthy to open the scroll or to look into it. Then one of the elders said to me, "Do not weep. See, the Lion of the tribe of Judah, the Root of David, has conquered, so that he can open the scroll and its seven seals."

Then I saw between the throne and the four living creatures and among the elders a Lamb standing as if it had been slaughtered, having seven horns and seven eyes, which are the seven spirits of God sent out into all the earth. He went and took the scroll from the right hand of the one who was seated on the throne. When he had taken the scroll, the four living creatures and the twenty-four elders fell before the Lamb, each holding a harp and golden bowls full of incense, which are the prayers of the saints. They sing a new song:

"You are worthy to take the scroll
and to open its seals,
for you were slaughtered and by your blood you ransomed for God
saints from every tribe and language and people and nation;
you have made them to be a kingdom and priests serving our God,
and they will reign on earth."

Then I looked, and I heard the voice of many angels surrounding the throne and the living creatures and the elders; they numbered myriads of myriads and thousands of thousands, singing with full voice,

"Worthy is the Lamb that was slaughtered
to receive power and wealth and wisdom and might
and honor and glory and blessing!"
Then I heard every creature in heaven and on earth and under the earth and in the sea, and all that is in them, singing,
"To the one seated on the throne and to the Lamb
be blessing and honor and glory and might
forever and ever!"
And the four living creatures said, "Amen!" And the elders fell down and worshiped.

So how does it all end? We humans keep asking that question from one generation to the next. In fact, the question is probably as old as the human race. Adults talk about it with a foreboding phrase, "the end of the world." Children have a more trusting mood. They put it into every bedtime story when they reach a point where they think they won't stay awake until the story is finished. "Tell me," they say to Mother or Father or babysitter, "tell me how the story ends."

I expect that one reason the New Testament book of Revelation is so perennially popular is because it tells us about the end. And as befits such a profound and mysterious subject, Revelation casts the endtime story in language as colorful as a surrealistic painting. The feeling of mystery in the book intrigues us, and sometimes frustrates us. We wish it would tell us how and when. *Especially* when! Instead, its language tantalizes our imagination. It's no wonder that preachers and Bible students of every style and stripe have ventured to explain it.

Nor is it any wonder that so many of these explanations (a huge majority, in fact) insist on finding the key to Revelation in their own time. I've watched two generations of earnest persons do this in my lifetime, but they are only the most recent descendants of a line that goes back centuries—probably to the very generation in which the book was written. Something in us *wants* the book to find its fulfillment in our time; at our best moments because we want to see "the new heaven and new earth" of which the book writes, and at our more vengeful moments because we think it's time for judgment to fall on the corruption that seems to engulf our world.

But we are in too much of a hurry, and we are too anxious to find the meaning of each jot and tittle. As a result, we move distractedly through the groves of wonder, missing the beauty, promise, and hope that flow so gloriously through the book.

Let there be no question about it, however: The book also has violence. A great deal of it. That shouldn't surprise us. As theologians (and you and I are theologians, because we think about God, the primary subject of theology; we may not be trained or professional theologians, but we're theologians, all the same), we have heard about sin, and we know that sin is violent at its heart. Even the smallest of our sins, such as our petty irritations and jealousies, carry an incipient quality of violence. Then, too, you and I have lived for a while, and anyone who has lived for a while has observed that violence exists in our world. So of course there will be violence in this book that reveals the final consummation of our world. Anything that has had so prominent a role in our human history must of course have prominence in the climax of our story.

But when the violence comes, it catches us unawares. Revelation begins with a dramatic picture of Jesus Christ, followed by open letters to the seven churches of Asia. Chapter four moves us into the sublime motif of worship that weaves all through the book. But this ecstasy is interrupted by an impasse. There is in the right hand of God a scroll of crucial importance (else why would it be in God's right hand), and no one is "worthy" to open the scroll or to break its seals. The eternal drama, which has now mounted to its climax, cannot proceed until the scroll is opened.

John, the conveyor of this wonderful book, begins to "weep bitterly." It's as if history has come not to an end, but—as I said earlier—to an impasse. Everything will stop here, unless someone can open this scroll, unless—specifically—someone is "worthy" to do so. But now a heavenly elder consoles John. "Do not weep. See, the Lion of the tribe of Judah, the Root of David, has conquered, so that he can open the scroll and its seven seals" (Revelation 5:5).

So the plot can now continue to unfold. A typical reader is not surprised; the "worthy" one is someone who has "conquered," and obviously a great conqueror will be needed for such an assignment as this.

For those who are familiar with the biblical story, the means of unfolding is just what might have been expected. The "Lion of Judah" and the "Root of David" are terms that had been significant in Jewish expectation for centuries. The Lion of Judah was a term going all the way back to Jacob's blessings on his sons (Genesis 49:8-12); the Root of David was tied to the root of Judah (2 Kings 19:30) and the root of Jesse, David's father (Isaiah 11:10), a kind of poetic shorthand for the kingly line in Judah's tribe that found its highest expression in King David. Both phrases were messianic terms, expressing the ancient dream and expectation of God's ultimate ruler who would someday appear. So when John hears that there is, indeed, a "worthy" one, he isn't surprised at who it is. Who else would it be but a conqueror, and who else but the one predicted by poets and prophets. And a *Lion*, of course! A dominant, regal, majestic figure, of the sort that could be expected to deal with the ultimates of history.

But now heaven plays one of its magnificent, wonderful jokes. As we brace ourselves for the appearance of this conquering Lion, accompanied by some celestial version of "Hail to the Chief" and with all proper panoply and display, we are greeted instead by "a Lamb standing as if it had been slaughtered" (Revelation 5:6). And there *is* music, but not exactly what we had expected to hear:

> "Worthy is the Lamb that was slaughtered
> to receive power and wealth and wisdom and might
> and honor and glory and blessing!"
>
> (REVELATION 5:12)

How odd of God, to think of a Lion as a Lamb! And how odd of God to picture the conqueror as a helpless, slaughtered thing. That is, how odd of God to work through a Cross.

In a sense, of course, the Lamb is not a complete surprise. That is, if you know the biblical story, you've heard before of the Lamb. There's a long heritage. When the death angel was to visit Egypt just prior to the exodus of the children of Israel, the Israelites were told to protect themselves from this death angel by sacrificing a lamb and sprinkling some of its blood on the doorposts of their homes. Thus it was a slain lamb that made war, so to speak, on the agent of death. Centuries later, when John the Baptist "introduced" Jesus to those who were with him—perhaps a throng, for all we know—it was with the phrase, "Here is the Lamb of God who takes away the sin of the world!" (John 1:29). So although the slain Lamb is an unlikely figure when we're expecting to see a Lion, the Lamb itself is a figure with a history.

But the surprises are not over. The Lamb, this slain creature, this symbol of meekness, will now unloose judgment on the earth. Layer upon layer of judgment. The scroll that must be opened is a scroll of judgment, unleashing seven seals—the first four of which are the fabled four horsemen of the apocalypse. We encounter scenes of famine, death, and calamities of nature so terrible that "the kings of the earth and the magnates and the generals and the rich and the powerful, and everyone, slave and free, hid in the caves and among the rocks of the mountains," crying for protection from (of all things), "the wrath of the Lamb" (Revelation 6:15-16).

If Revelation were not such a serious book, a person would conclude that the writer is engaged in some kind of absurd humor. It seems like a cartoon-comic scene: The most powerful figures, from the palaces and White House of earth to the corporate boardrooms, are running in terror because a lamb is pursuing them! A lamb full of wrath! Still more ludicrous, this is a lamb that has been slain; it is a bruised, bloody, beaten thing.

As we read on in the book of Revelation, we get the feeling that the suffering of this lamb represents not only Jesus, the Lamb of God, but perhaps all of the persons through the ages who have suffered and died for their loyalty to God. A multitude beyond counting appears before the throne of God and of the Lamb, praising God, and when an observer asks about this multitude, we learn that they are those "who have come out of the great ordeal" (Revelation 7:14). And again, the Lamb is the issue: "They have washed their robes and made them white in the blood of the Lamb," and "the Lamb at the center of the throne will be their shepherd" (Revelation 7:14, 17).

The Lamb continues to be the key figure through the rest of this strange and wonderful book of Revelation. And perhaps I should say that, strange and wonderful as all of this book is, nothing is more so than the fact that it revolves around the slain Lamb! Much of the speculating, preaching, and imagining about Revelation centers on its horror, and certainly with some reason. But this symphony has one dominant motif, and it surfaces repeatedly, in every kind of time and place. The heart of the symphony is the slain lamb.

So it is, then, that the persons who take the "mark of the beast" will be "tormented . . . in the presence of the holy angels and in the presence of the Lamb" (Revelation 14:10). When the forces of total evil "make war," it is on the Lamb; but "the Lamb will conquer them, for he is Lord of lords and King of kings" (Revelation 17:14). When the divine triumph is celebrated, it will be at "the marriage supper of the Lamb" (Revelation 19:9); and as for the wonderful holy city, there will be no temple there, and no need of sun or moon, because the "temple is the Lord God the Almighty and the Lamb," and the city's "lamp is the Lamb"

(Revelation 21:22-23). And of course the throne upon which everything centers in that eternal setting is "the throne of God and of the Lamb" (Revelation 22:1, 3).

All of which only underscores our surprise, the surprise that has become our problem. When, early in the Revelation story, we saw heaven at a standstill because no one was worthy to open the book of the story of God, and we were told that the Lion of Judah would be able to do so, and then a slain Lamb appeared, we were taken by cosmic surprise. But as the plot continues to unfold, we discover that this is no fluke; the Lamb really is the central character. How can this be? We can understand a Lion—but a Lamb?

But, of course, this is how we miss God, and God's will and purposes, all along. We believe in this poor, transient power that struts and poses so regularly on the world's stage. We talk about armed might and ballistic missiles; about gross national product and corporate power; about the television sound bytes that shape public opinion polls. These are our lions. And it's easy to understand our outlook, because all of these things give every evidence of power. It was in our generation that people first began saying, "If you've got it, flaunt it," but every generation since the beginning has believed and practiced it. We believe in the lion, the obvious power, and we have, ever since we bit into the forbidden fruit.

But God, contrary to all of our logic, says that the power is in a Lamb, and a *slain* Lamb at that. God so loved the world that he *gave*. Did not command, did not assert divine authority, did not overpower, but pleased in the most helpless fashion, by giving the eternal Son, the Lamb.

So of course God asks us to follow in the same mood. We are instructed that it is better to give than to receive, told that we should wash feet, advised that it is blessed to be a servant. But we don't believe it. Not really. We stand in awe of Francis of Assisi, Harry Denman, Mother Teresa, and a countless host of lesser-known persons who have chosen the way of the Lamb, but we invest our money in our public relations campaigns and our pursuit of power. We find it very hard to believe that it pays to wash feet, to lay down our lives, to carry a cross. The cross is a lovely piece of jewelry, but an ugly burden.

But I remind you that Revelation isn't finished shocking us when it shows us that God's Lion is a Lamb. More startling still, the Lamb opens the book of judgment. Reynolds Price, the novelist with a bent toward theology, observes that the Palm Sunday throngs didn't fully understand the peaceful Messiah, because "they misconstrue his mildness" (*Three Gospels*, 51). Charles Rann Kennedy, the British playwright, described Jesus and his followers as "The Terrible Meek," because "all the empires can't kill him" (*Plays for Seven Players*, 632).

Because of course there is wrath in love. Wrath that strikes at the pit of the stomach and eats at the very marrow of our bones. When I have done wrong, I would rather stand a thousand times in the face of bitter anger than in the presence of broken love. I don't know how it is that the wrath of the Lamb works; I don't profess to understand the details of the monstrous judgments that unfold when the Lamb opens the vaults of judgment in Revelation. I only know that it is the judgment of love, and I cannot think of anything more terrifying to creatures who have a capacity for receiving love than to face the love they have violated. I think that the language of judgment—the famine and pestilence, the sun black as sackcloth and the moon like blood, the bloody seas and the falling stars—are symbolic, because the true wrath of love is more than our mortal minds can conceive of.

But make no mistake of it. God's method is love, his vehicle is a slain Lamb, and his call is to a cross. It is no idle chance that the controlling motif of the book of Revelation is a Lamb that has been slaughtered. This slain Lamb is the key to history, and to its glorious consummation.

And yes, the Lamb is a Lion. This may be the most important thing to know about the book of Revelation. And about life, as well.

New Testament Stories from the Back Side

Written by John D. Schroeder

*N*ew Testament Stories from the Back Side is a collection of essays designed to stimulate our thinking and give us a fresh perspective about twelve stories from the New Testament. This study guide is intended to assist you in facilitating a study or discussion group, so that the experience is beneficial for all. Here are some thoughts on how you can help your group.

SUGGESTIONS FOR LEADERS

1. Distribute the book to participants before your first group meeting and request that they read the introduction prior to the meeting. You may want to limit the size of your group to increase each member's opportunity for more in-depth participation.

2. Participants may ask what the title of the book means. The "back side" simply means a different perspective in order to gain new insights about ourselves, others, and our faith.

3. Begin your group meetings or sessions on time. Participants will appreciate your promptness. You may want to begin your first session with introductions and a brief get-acquainted time. Start each session by reading aloud the snapshot summary of the chapter for the day.

4. Select discussion questions and activities in advance. Note that the first question is usually a general question designed

to get the discussion going. Feel free to change the order of the questions as listed and/or to create your own questions. Allow a specified time for the questions and activities.

5. Remind participants that all questions are valid as part of the learning process. Encourage their participation in discussion by informing that there are no "wrong" answers and that all input will be appreciated. Invite participants to share their thoughts, personal stories, and ideas as their comfort level dictates.

6. Some questions may be more difficult to answer than others. If you ask a question and no one responds, begin the discussion by venturing an answer yourself. Then ask for comments and other answers. Remember that some questions may have multiple answers.

7. Ask the questions "Why?" or "Why do you believe that?" to help continue a discussion and give it greater depth.

8. Give everyone a chance to talk. Keep the conversation moving. Occasionally you may want to direct a question at a specific person who has not spoken up. Asking, "Do you have anything to add?" or "What do *you* think?" may be a way to invite participation in a nonthreatening way. If the conversation veers too far away from the main topic, move ahead by asking the next question.

9. Before moving from questions to activities, ask participants if they have any questions that have not been answered. Remember that as a leader, you do not have to know all the answers. Some answers may come from group members. Other answers may even need a bit of research. Your job is to keep the discussion moving and to encourage participation.

10. Review the activity in advance. Feel free to modify it or create your own activity. Encourage participants to try the "At home" activity.

11. Following the conclusion of the activity, close with a brief prayer, either the prayer suggested in the study guide

or one of your own. If your group desires, pause for individual prayer petitions.

12. Be grateful and supportive. Thank members for their ideas and participation.

13. You are not expected to be a "perfect" leader. Just do the best you can by focusing on the participants and the lesson. God will help you lead this group.

14. Enjoy your time together.

SUGGESTIONS FOR PARTICIPANTS

1. What you will receive from this study will be in direct proportion to your involvement. Be an active participant.

2. Please make a point to attend all sessions and to arrive on time so that you receive the greatest benefit.

3. Read the lesson and review the questions prior to the meeting. You may want to jot down questions you have from the reading and also answers to some of the study guide questions.

4. Be supportive and appreciative of your group leader as well as the other members of the group. You are on a journey together.

5. Your participation is encouraged. Feel free to share your thoughts about the material being discussed.

6. Pray for your group and your group leader.

CHAPTER 1: BABY PICTURES

Luke 2:22-38

Snapshot Summary

This first chapter gives us pictures of Jesus as an infant and shows us the true meaning of Christmas.

Discussion Questions

1. What insights did you receive from this chapter?

2. Why do we treasure baby pictures?

3. How does it feel to show pictures? How does it feel to be shown them?

4. What do we learn from Luke's two pictures?

5. How is Matthew's picture different from Luke's two pictures?

6. What do these pictures reveal about Jesus?

7. How are they different from ordinary pictures?

8. What is typical about Jesus' birth and his early baby pictures?

9. Discuss the baby pictures John provides in John 1:14.

10. How do our pictures of Christmas differ from God's reason for the first Christmas?

Activities

As a group: Brainstorm ideas on how to celebrate the real meaning of Christmas.

At home: Read the Christmas story with someone and discuss what it means for us today.

Prayer: Dear God, we thank you for showing us pictures of Jesus' life and for opening our eyes to the real meaning of Christmas. May we celebrate your many gifts each day of the year. Amen.

CHAPTER 2: MARY SHOULDN'T HAVE WORRIED

Luke 2:39-51

Snapshot Summary

This chapter examines the Bible's only anecdote of Jesus' boyhood.

Discussion Questions

1. What new insights did you receive from this chapter?

2. Why do you think the Bible does not include any other stories from Jesus' boyhood years?

3. Why was this story included? What does it tell us?

4. What is so fascinating about Jesus' response to his mother?

5. How is this story both reassuring and frightening?

6. What human elements are contained in this story?

7. What is the "basic rule" of raising children, according to the author?

8. What lessons can parents learn from this story?

9. In what ways do parents influence their children?

10. What are the other influences on children today?

Activities

As a group: Discuss your childhood influences.

At home: Be aware of how you influence others, especially children, during this coming week.

Prayer: God, we thank you for those who influenced us to attend church and learn about you. May we be your voice and arms during the coming week. Amen.

CHAPTER 3: LISTEN TO THE WIND

John 3:1-8

Snapshot Summary

This chapter examines the discussion between Jesus and Nicodemus, and shows us how the Holy Spirit is like the wind.

Discussion Questions

1. What insights did you receive from this chapter?

2. In what ways do we try to put boundaries on God?

3. Recall a time that you tried to box God in. What were the results?

4. Why do you think Nicodemus sought out Jesus?

5. What did Jesus want Nicodemus to understand?

6. Can we shut out the Spirit? By what activities?

7. What happens when we listen to the Spirit of God?

8. How did the Spirit influence the later actions of Nicodemus?

9. How is the Spirit of God like the wind?

10. What are the major points of this lesson?

Activities

As a group: Share your knowledge and questions about the Holy Spirit.

At home: When you feel the wind this week, remember God's Holy Spirit.

Prayer: Jesus, we thank you that your Holy Spirit lives in us and in all believers. Help us to listen to your Spirit and serve you faithfully. Amen.

CHAPTER 4: IN DEFENSE OF A MAN I DON'T LIKE

John 5:2-16

Snapshot Summary

This chapter helps us understand people we may not like through the example of Jesus healing the man at the pool.

Discussion Questions

1. What insights did you receive from this chapter?

2. What are common traits that make people unappealing?

3. Recall someone you didn't like initially who is now a good friend.

4. Could you defend someone you didn't like? Explain.

5. What does the author find unappealing about the man in the story?

6. Why do you think Jesus healed the man?

7. Do you feel sorry for this man? Explain.

8. What does this story tell you of Jesus' love and his grace?

9. How would being completely dependent on others change your life?

10. How do people today become "programmed to lose"?

Activities

As a group: You have been assigned to befriend a convicted murderer in prison. Discuss your feelings.

At home: Take a fresh look this week at a person you don't care for and try to see the person Jesus does.

Prayer: Jesus, give us your eyes to see others as you see them. May we grow in your grace to love our neighbors. Amen.

CHAPTER 5: A WILD AND WONDERFUL WOMAN

John 4:7-18, 28-30

Snapshot Summary

This chapter examines Jesus' encounter with the woman at the well in Samaria. It shows the transforming power of meeting Jesus.

Discussion Questions

1. What new insights did you receive from this chapter?

2. Why do you think Jesus asked for a drink of water?

3. What was unusual about this woman from other local women?

4. What are some facts that define people to others? What fact would define you or someone you know?

5. Do you think their meeting was divine providence? Why or why not?

6. How was her life changed by this meeting and conversation with Jesus?

7. What were the religious differences between Jesus and the woman?

8. What do you think made her testimony about Jesus so effective?

9. Why do you think Jesus said to her, "I am he"?

10. What is the author's formula for starting a church?

Activities

As a group: Recall a meeting or conversation with someone that changed your life or that of someone you know.

At home: Pray for churches that are just being started.

Prayer: Jesus, we thank you for your transforming power that changes us and changes the lives of others. Help us to share the good news of your love. Amen.

CHAPTER 6: THE IMPORTANCE OF BEING BILINGUAL

Mark 10:46-52

Snapshot Summary

This chapter takes a fresh look at the story of Bartimaeus, a blind beggar who used his second language to gain his sight from Jesus.

Discussion Questions

1. What insights did you receive from this chapter?

2. How important do you think it is to know a second language? Why?

3. What liabilities did Bartimaeus have? What were his assets?

4. How did Bartimaeus gain Jesus' attention?

5. What was so eloquent about Bartimaeus's prayer?

6. Why does prayer come natural to all humans?

7. What does the author say about the importance of knowing how to pray?

8. How is divine eloquence within everyone's reach?

9. How does passionate need make a prayer more effective?

10. What is the major point of this lesson?

Activities

As a group: Share what prayer and the power of prayer means to you.

At home: Focus on improving your prayer life this week.

Prayer: Lord, teach us to pray that we may talk to you and hear what you have to say to us. Thank you for the gift of prayer and help us to pray with confidence. Amen.

CHAPTER 7: EXPECTING A LITTLE KING

Mark 11:1-10

Snapshot Summary

This chapter examines the first Palm Sunday and the expectations of the crowd who cheered Jesus.

Discussion Questions

1. What new insights did you receive from this chapter?

2. Share some of your childhood memories of Palm Sunday.

3. Why do you think Jesus chose a donkey?

4. When the crowds cried "Hosanna!" what were they saying?

5. What did the crowds want from Jesus?

6. What was the gentle strength of Jesus on that first Palm Sunday?

7. Why were the expectations of the crowd too small?

8. Why did the crowd see a little king?

9. How do we often choose a little king?

10. What is the coming "new Palm Sunday"?

Activities

As a group: Discuss the benefits and price of belonging to God's kingdom.

At home: Meditate on what you expect of Jesus and what Jesus expects of you.

Prayer: Jesus, open our eyes so we see the bigger picture of you, your kingdom, and your love. Thank you for your many gifts and your constant presence. Amen.

CHAPTER 8: ONCE THERE WAS A TABLE

Luke 22:7-23

Snapshot Summary

This chapter looks at a very special table: the Lord's Table and the first Holy Communion.

Discussion Questions

1. What insights did you receive from this chapter?

2. Describe your favorite table or a table experience from childhood.

3. How important were tables in the time of Jesus?

4. Describe the conversation/argument of the disciples before the Last Supper.

5. What did Jesus tell them about greatness?

6. How did Jesus bring a whole new meaning to the word "table"?

7. Why do you think the disciples remembered the first communion experience?

8. Recall a meaningful communion experience.

9. Why do we often leave the communion table without realizing the magnitude of what has happened?

10. How far does the Holy Communion table reach?

Activities

As a group: Share Holy Communion as a group gathered around a table.

At home: Meditate about Holy Communion.

Prayer: God, we thank you for the gift of Holy Communion. Help us to treasure this gift and use it to grow closer to you. Amen.

CHAPTER 9: THE FULL TOMB

John 20:1-18

Snapshot Summary

This chapter looks at the Easter story from the viewpoint of the full tomb and what it means for us today.

Discussion Questions

1. What insights did you receive from this chapter?

2. Name some symbols of Easter.

3. Why would an empty tomb normally be forgotten?

4. How did Jesus fill the tomb?

5. Why does the author say the tomb is full rather than empty?

6. Why is the tomb symbolic of all that Easter means?

7. How does the tomb symbolize hope and victory?

8. Why were the odds so against the first believers?

9. How does fullness make a difference in believers?

10. How do holy shrines illustrate how full the tomb is?

Activities

As a group: Visit a local cemetery and note expressions and symbols of hope.

At home: Share the lesson of the full tomb with someone this week.

Prayer: God, we thank you for Easter and what it means for us and our eternal future. Help us to share the news of your full tomb with others. Amen.

CHAPTER 10: AT THE CORNER OF TODAY AND FOREVER

Acts 16:16-34

Snapshot Summary

This chapter illustrates how life can change in an instant, as seen through the eyes of a Roman jailer.

Discussion Questions

1. What insights did you receive from this chapter?

2. In your own words, tell what the title of this lesson means to you.

3. Would you like to be warned of dangerous intersections in life? Why?

4. When did you first feel that you matter to God?

5. Recall an encounter that was life changing.

6. What kind of man was the jailer before and after his experience?

7. What was so different about the jailer's two prisoners?

8. How does eternity begin today?

9. Name some incidents that can change a person's life.

10. What is the main point of this lesson?

Activities

As a group: Discuss the author's statement that "everything that happens to us has some possible significance for eternity."

At home: Pray for someone you know or someone in the news who is at a dangerous intersection.

Prayer: Lord, thank you for being with us through all the dangerous intersections in life. Help us remember your faithfulness and love. Amen.

CHAPTER 11: GOING EASTER SHOPPING

Colossians 3:5-14

Snapshot Summary

This chapter shows us what traits and behavior are in fashion for Christians through a visit to the Resurrection Shop.

Discussion Questions

1. What new insights did you receive from this chapter?

2. What does the author mean by spiritual garments? Give some examples.

3. What does it cost to wear spiritual garments?

4. What does the author mean by the Resurrection Shop?

5. How are standards different at the Resurrection Shop? Who are you compared to?

6. What completes the resurrection wardrobe? Why?

7. Why is one trip not enough to the Resurrection Shop?

8. What does Paul encourage us to eliminate from our life?

9. What traits does Paul encourage us to get and keep?

10. What happens when you take off your old robe and put on the new?

Activities

As a group: Discuss spiritual garments worn by others that have influenced your life.

At home: Comment on someone's spiritual wardrobe this week.

Prayer: God, clothe us in the traits and attitudes that point others to you. Thank you for the resurrection that makes it all possible. Amen.

CHAPTER 12: THE LION AND THE LAMB

Revelation 5:1-14

Snapshot Summary

This final chapter deals with the end of the world as revealed in the book of Revelation through the key figures of the Lion and the Lamb.

Discussion Questions

1. What insights did you receive from this chapter?

2. Why are humans so fascinated about how things end?

3. Share your favorite ending to a book or story.

4. Why is the book of Revelation so hard to understand?

5. What surprises does Revelation contain?

6. What feelings do you get in reading Revelation?

7. What do you know about the Lamb, the key figure in Revelation?

8. How is God's world different from our world?

9. What does Revelation tell us of God's love?

10. What part do we as Christians play in Revelation?

Activities

As a group: Share what you have gained through this series of discussions.

At home: Remember the members of this group in your prayers.

Prayer: God, thank you for giving us this time together to learn more about you and ourselves. Be with us as we go our separate ways and continue to encourage us with your love. Amen.